Jesus, Debt, and the Lord's Prayer

Jesus, Debt, and the Lord's Prayer

First-Century Debt
and Jesus' Intentions

Douglas E. Oakman

©

James Clarke & Co

James Clarke & Co
P.O. Box 60
Cambridge
CB1 2NT
United Kingdom

www.jamesclarke.co
publishing@jamesclarke.co

ISBN: 978 0 227 17529 3

British Library Cataloguing in Publication Data
A record is available from the British Library

First published by James Clarke & Co, 2015

Copyright © Douglas E. Oakman, 2014

Published by arrangement
with Cascade Books

For my dear grandchildren
Sarah, Sophia, Samuel, and Cora

A certain creditor had two debtors;

one owed five hundred *denarii*, and the other fifty.

When they could not pay,

he canceled the debts for both of them.

Now which of them will love him more?"

Simon answered,

"I suppose the one for whom he canceled the greater debt."

And Jesus said to him,

"You have judged rightly."

—LUKE 7:41–43

Contents

Foreword

The complexity of ancient economics (taxes, loans, debts, sureties, trade, markets) seems on its face to have little to do with Jesus and his prayer. But Doug Oakman's work—not only in this volume, but in his work over the past thirty years—has shown that these issues are fundamental to understanding what Jesus was up to, what his central concerns were, and what the problems were that he addressed in many of his sayings and parables.

What Oakman does here is to bring to the reader's attention the economic issues that plagued first-century Galilean and Judean peasants in their agrarian world. The issues of indebtedness, loss of land, and heavy taxation loomed large, and the urban elites—in Rome, Jerusalem, Tiberias, and elsewhere—could benefit greatly in this system. What Oakman does so well is to move from the details of the larger picture regarding the systemic structures and historical events and players to the ways in which Jesus articulated a response to them.

The bookshelves are crowded with volumes old and new studying the historical Jesus and his sayings, and some of them, in my estimation, are very good. But most of what one finds on those shelves is either a tweaking of older approaches or the repetition of pious platitudes about Jesus. What Oakman offers in these brief chapters is a fresh look at some of the core sayings of Jesus, including the Lord's Prayer, with a view to the economic situation of first-century Galilee and Judea.

How would what Jesus says to those who heard him speak sound differently if we seriously listened to and understood the implications of debt, the huge gap between peasants and urban elites, and the heavy burden of tax obligations in that society?

Jesus was not crucified because he taught pious platitudes—who would have cared? He was not crucified because he had a different take on traditional Israelite law—lots of Judean teachers of his day and later had major disagreements on these issues. He was crucified because what he had to say was perceived as a fundamental challenge to the status quo, and that included his comments on debt and taxation.

Oakman does not claim to have the last word on the Jesus traditions. What he does offer, however, is a challenge to take seriously the economic and broad social implications of what Jesus had to say. Personally, I cannot read the gospels the same way after reading Oakman's work.

—K. C. Hanson

Preface

. . . if coined money emancipated the small producer from one set of masters, it threatened to hand him over to another just as money in general had done. Usury, mortgages and enslaved debtors followed the new medium of exchange wherever it was introduced.

—V. GORDON CHILDE[1]

The following essays are linked by an important theme in the history of Jesus. The Q reference to debt prison (Luke 12:58–59),[2] the stories of the Two Debtors or the Unjust Steward in Luke, the parable of the Unforgiving Slave in Matthew, or the Prayer of Jesus, also known as the Lord's Prayer, along with much other good Jesus material, suggest that he had a central material concern for contemporaries who were in debt. The Prayer especially shows direct interest in the alleviation or mitigation of agrarian money debts. Very early references in the Jesus tradition to eating with tax collectors and "sinners" reflect a praxis that aimed to alleviate the oppression of the indebted.

The Babatha Archives, and traditions about the prozbul of Hillel or the burning of the Jerusalem Archives by the insurgents in 66 CE, provide evidence external to the Jesus traditions for the importance of money loans and social problems created by debt in Roman Judea.[3]

1. Childe, *What Happened in History*, 202.

2. Q refers to the earliest collection of Jesus' sayings and by convention is cited by their location in the Gospel of Luke.

3. Goodman, "The First Jewish Revolt."

For Galilee, Josephus mentions the royal bank and archives at Sepphoris and popular hatred of Sepphoris for its allegiance to Rome.[4] The Roman Overlord encouraged money loans and provincial mints in order to enhance social control through relations of indebtedness. Debts were probably more effective at provincial control than the Roman legions!

Modern denizens, of course, also know indebtedness. The prevalence of "plastic money," and the fact that money loans by private banks actually create "money," lend some insight into such relations today.[5]

U.S. household consumer debt profile:
>   Average credit card debt: $15,191
>   Average mortgage debt: $154,365
>   Average student loan debt: $33,607

In total, American consumers owe as of April 2014:
> $11.68 trillion in debt
>   An increase of 3.7% from last year
> $854.2 billion in credit card debt
> $8.15 trillion in mortgages
> $1,115.3 billion in student loans
>   An increase of 13.9% from last year

In modern capitalism, loans-at-interest are the basis for "growth." However, market capitalism at home and worldwide has taken on an ominous imbalance. OxFam International recently reported:

> Given the scale of rising wealth concentrations, opportunity capture and unequal political representation are a serious and worrying trend. For instance:
> • Almost half of the world's wealth is now owned by just one percent of the population.

---

4. Josephus, *Life* 38–39. Fiensy, *Christian Origins and the Ancient Economy,* 59–66, disputes this picture of wide-spread indebtedness.

5. Chen, "American Household Credit Card Debt Statistics: 2014"; see also Frizell, "Americans Are Taking on Debt at Scary High Rates." On creation of money through private banks, see Daly and Cobb, *For the Common Good,* 407.

- The wealth of the one percent richest people in the world amounts to $110 trillion. That's 65 times the total wealth of the bottom half of the world's population.

- The bottom half of the world's population owns the same as the richest 85 people in the world.

- Seven out of ten people live in countries where economic inequality has increased in the last 30 years.

- The richest one percent increased their share of income in 24 out of 26 countries for which we have data between 1980 and 2012.

- In the US, the wealthiest one percent captured 95 percent of post-financial crisis growth since 2009, while the bottom 90 percent became poorer.[6]

Thomas Piketty's recent analysis of capital and capitalism has created a contemporary stir on both the left and the right:

> Modern economic growth and the diffusion of knowledge have made it possible to avoid the Marxist apocalypse but have not modified the deep structures of capital and inequality—or in any case not as much as one might have imagined in the optimistic decades following World War II. When the rate of return on capital exceeds the rate of growth of output and income, as it did in the nineteenth century and seems quite likely to do again in the twenty-first, capitalism automatically generates arbitrary and unsustainable inequalities that radically undermine the meritocratic vales on which democratic societies are based.[7]

Pope Francis likewise expressed moral concern about modern economic disparity in his recent exhortation *Evangelii Gaudium*, "The Joy of the Gospel":

> While the earnings of a minority are growing exponentially, so too is the gap separating the majority from the prosperity enjoyed by those happy few. This imbalance

6. Further details found in Oxfam, *Working for the Few*; see also D. Smith, *The Penguin State of the World Atlas*.

7. Piketty, *Capital in the Twenty-first Century*, 1.

is the result of ideologies which defend the absolute autonomy of the marketplace and financial speculation. Consequently, they reject the right of states, charged with vigilance for the common good, to exercise any form of control. A new tyranny is thus born, invisible and often virtual, which unilaterally and relentlessly imposes its own laws and rules. Debt and the accumulation of interest also make it difficult for countries to realize the potential of their own economies and keep citizens from enjoying their real purchasing power.[8]

David Graeber recently has provided an important historical survey of the phenomenon of debt. Its social mortgage has as often been negative as constructive. One passage in Graeber's book is particularly striking:

> For thousands of years, the struggle between rich and poor has largely taken the form of conflicts between creditors and debtors—of arguments about the rights and wrongs of interest payments, debt peonage, amnesty, repossession, restitution, the sequestering of sheep, the seizing of vineyards, and the selling of debtors' children into slavery. By the same token, for the last five thousand years, with remarkable regularity, popular insurrections have begun the same way: with the ritual destruction of the debt records—tablets, papyri, ledgers, whatever form they might have taken in any particular time and place. (After that, rebels usually go after the records of landholding and tax assessments.) As the great classicist Moses Finley often liked to say, in the ancient world, all revolutionary movements had a single program: "Cancel the debts and redistribute the land."[9]

In this *libellus*, then, I attempt to give several previous essays a more integral focus on Jesus and Debt. The important theme of liberation from debt is close to the heart of Jesus' historical significance. Yet the implications are also deeply theological and christological. The good news of redemption is not simply an otherworldly chimera.

8. Pope Francis, *Apostolic Exhortation Evangelii Gaudium*, §56.

9. Graeber, *Debt*, 8

Redemption from debt slavery is a central metaphor in the Bible. Perhaps these essays will find use in classrooms and reading groups, and help readers to think about the consequences of a world in debt, and of the many as a consequence in a world of hurt. It was after all Jesus who said, "You cannot serve God and Mammon."[10]

10. Luke 16:13 [Q]. Mammon refers to wealth trusted for material security such as money on loan or storehouses. Consider Luke 12:16–20.

Acknowledgments

With the exception of chapter 1, the following chapters are revised versions of previously published articles and are reprinted with permission of the publishers. The author and publisher gratefully acknowledge the cooperation of these publishers.

Chapter 2, "Jesus and Agrarian Palestine: The Factor of Debt," was first published in *Society of Biblical Literature 1985 Seminar Papers*, edited by Kent Harold Richards, 57–73. Atlanta: Scholars, 1985. It also appeared in Oakman, *Jesus and the Peasants*, 11–32. Matrix. Eugene, OR: Cascade Books, 2008. The version in this volume also includes elements from "Jesus and the Problem of Debt," first published in Oakman, *Jesus and the Peasants*, 33–39.

Chapter 3, "The Lord's Prayer in Social Perspective," was first published in *Authenticating the Words of Jesus*, edited by Bruce Chilton and Craig A. Evans, 137–86. New Testament Tools and Studies 28.1. Leiden: Brill, 1999. It also appeared in Oakman, *Jesus and the Peasants*, 119–249.

Chapter 4, "Jesus the Tax Resister," was first published in Oakman, *Jesus and the Peasants*, 280–97.

Conclusion includes verbatim paragraphs that were first published in "Biblical Economics in an Age of Greed," in *Market and Margins: Lutheran Perspectives*, edited by Wanda Deifelt, 82–97. Minneapolis: Lutheran University Press, 2014.

Abbreviations

Ant.	Josephus, *Antiquities of the Judeans*
b.	Babylonian Talmud
BAGD	W. Bauer, W. F. Arndt, F. W. Gingrich, and F. W. Danker, *A Greek-English Lexicon of the New Testament and Other Christian Literature*
BCE	Before the Common Era
BDB	F. Brown, S. R. Driver, C. A. Briggs, *Hebrew English Lexicon of the Old Testament*
BDF	F. Blass, A. Debrunner, and R. W. Funk, *A Greek Grammar of the New Testament and Other Early Christian Literature*
Cant. Rab.	*Canticles Rabbah*
CD	Damascus Document
CE	Common Era
CIL	*Corpus Inscriptionum Latinarum*
Eccl. Rab.	*Ecclesiastes Rabbah*
Exod. Rab.	*Exodus Rabbah*
Ezek. Trag.	*Ezekiel the Tragedian*
Gen. Rab.	*Genesis Rabbah*
GThom	*Gospel of Thomas*
L	the material unique to the Gospel of Luke
Lam. Rab.	*Lamentations Rabbah*

LCL	Loeb Classical Library
Lev. Rab.	*Leviticus Rabbah*
Life	Josephus, *The Life*
LSJ	H. G. Liddel, R. Scott, H. S. Jones, *A Greek-English Lexicon with a Supplement*
m.	Mishnah
M	the material unique to the Gospel of Matthew
NRSV	New Revised Standard Version
Num. Rab.	*Numbers Rabbah*
par.	parallel passages in other Synoptic Gospels
OGIS	*Orientis Graeci Inscriptiones Selectae*
Q	Sayings Gospel, a literary source of Matthew and Luke
Q^1	the earliest layer of Q—Wisdom Q
Q^2	the second layer of Q—Deuteronomic Q
RSV	Revised Standard Version
Ruth Rab.	*Ruth Rabbah*
SEHHW	Rostovtzeff, *The Social and Economic History of the Hellenistic World*
SEHRW	Rostovtzeff, *The Social and Economic History of the Roman World*
Spec. Laws	Philo, *Special Laws*
Str.-B.	H. L. Strack and P. Billerbeck, *Kommentar zum Neuen Testament aus Talmud und Midrasch*
War	Josephus, *The Judean War*
y.	Jerusalem Talmud

CHAPTER 1

Introduction

Two Kingdoms, One Table—Jesus in Political Perspective

In the first century of the Common Era, two kingdoms were associated with Jesus of Nazareth.[1] Historically, he had proclaimed the Kingdom of God; to his followers posthumously, he would come into his own kingdom, the eternal kingdom of Jesus Christ. These two kingdoms had very different significance in regard to the meaning of Jesus' own historical activity and, later, in relationship to the political ethos of Christianity.

Imagine with me a triptych, that is, a three-paneled depiction of Jesus and his significance. This type of art often appears in churches; it sometimes hangs in university libraries or museum galleries. The first panel represented in Fig. 1.1, the one on the right under the aspect of God's Kingdom, presents Jesus' profound care and compassion for those in need, especially those who were sick and without food. The second panel, the one on the left under the aspect of the eternal kingdom of Jesus Christ, shows what happened to his politics in the development of Christianity. Finally, the last panel, the center panel, focuses our attention on his enduring table and political vision.

1. This chapter originated as a lecture: first delivered for a Lutheran Studies Conference "What Has God to Do With Caesar? Lutheran Perspectives on Political Life," Pacific Lutheran University, Tacoma, Washington, 2012, then given as an Edgar Goodspeed Endowed Lecture, Denison University, Granville, Ohio, March 2014.

1

Panel One

So, panel one. Jesus was born during the earliest years of the Roman Principate, during the reign of the first Roman emperor Caesar Augustus (27 BCE—14 CE) and toward the end of the reign of the Roman client ruler Herod the Great (37–4 BCE). Jesus came into an agrarian world stressed by dramatic political changes—notably the integration of provincial areas into the Roman political-economic orbit, with consequent urbanization of eastern provincial areas, increase of patronage politics practiced by Roman elites, and commercialization of agrarian economic relations.

Figure 1.1: PANEL ONE

GOD'S KINGDOM AND JESUS

† Jesus' humble origins

† A commoner, a peasant artisan, a sociable man

† His praxis of brokering the Power

† Politics of subsistence, healing and mealing

† Herodian Galilee: Roman patronage politics, commercialization, urbanization

† The politics of subsistence: Five loaves and two fish

† Jesus' peasant theology, the presence of the Power

† Tax resistence, debt forgiveness, violation of the Roman order, risky business

> Luke 14:27 (Q^1, the earliest level of sayings of Jesus): The one who does not take one's cross and follow after me cannot be my disciple.

† Crucifixion as a (social) bandit

> Mark 15:27: And with him they crucified two bandits, one on his right and one on his left.

Critical scholarly argument makes clear that Jesus was likely born in Nazareth of Galilee. Nazareth was a very tiny village, near the Galilean city of Sepphoris. Our earliest witness Paul simply says "born of a woman, born under the law" (Gal 4:4), though Paul says hardly anything about the life of the historical Jesus.[2] Mark 6 implies that Nazareth was Jesus' hometown, and Matt 21:11 and John 1:45 so identify him. The Sayings Gospel Q, the earliest substantial collection of material we have about Jesus, says nothing about his origins.

Moreover, Jesus' peasant birth without secure paternity (the son of Mary! Mark 6:3) and his wanderings as a peasant artisan, indicate his very low social status and honor rating in the eyes of his contemporaries. In fact, the dishonorable origins and dishonorable end of Jesus posed a significant challenge to the apostolic generation and evangelists, who needed to link Jesus solidly to Israelite prophecy, invent genealogies, and write apologetic passion stories in order to rescue Jesus' social status and honor. Paul shows the problem clearly in Gal 3:13; the Roman cross was a curse upon the memory of Jesus and a political liability for the earliest Christians. Theologically, Paul had to see that Jesus identified completely and wholly with the accursed of the earth, and Paul proclaimed that God had vindicated Jesus by raising him from the dead. The earliest identification of Jesus as the Christ stands in this vindication of Jesus' honor by God.

Otherwise, he was a commoner, through and through. And his identification and sympathy with commoners—fishers, farmers, prostitutes, the demon-possessed, social outcasts—seems to have been an expression of his enormous compassion for little people. It was on their behalf that he began a praxis of healing and mealing that would also be an expression of his brokering or mediating of the Power, the Kingdom of God, on behalf of the have-nots. But in order to do this, he became very good at ingratiating himself with those who had, and his parables show his wide-ranging social experience (probably garnered through his travels to where work could be had) and his skill at being invited to meals with the haves. Zacchaeus, though fictional, stands as a typical recollection of both Jesus' mealing and his wealing of "those without," after Zacchaeus is persuaded to return the take from the farmed taxes.

2. Biblical translations in this volume mostly follow the NRSV; on occasion, the translations are my own.

The "politics of Jesus" in my account, then, have to do centrally with what all peasants worry about—subsistence, daily and annually—and finessing the threats to subsistence. Peasants everywhere work the land and consume its produce. Who is a peasant? One who opens the front door and sees the entire year's food-supply in the yard and the fields. The harvest will not come easily, and the entire peasant family will participate in the daily and annual work-routines. Surplus adult peasant children, without secure access to their own land, will "hire out" or engage in other productive activities like the building trade or fishing. With preindustrial conditions of production, food storage is a problem and secure subsistence difficult to come by. Natural disasters like drought or pestilence are well known in biblical traditions (e.g., Joel); but equally important were predatory social relations.

Urbanization and commercialization of agrarian relations put much stress upon peasantry: absentee landlords owning large estates drive traditional peasants into tenancy or off the land altogether; commercialization leads to the production of agrarian products that do not serve the peasant family's daily or annual food needs.

The five loaves and two fish in the gospels are close to the daily subsistence needs of a family.[3] Tax collectors abound as elites seek a share in the peasantry's so-called surplus. Landlords living afar off, controlling large estates, lose touch with the conditions in the villages. Taxes and rents, unable to be paid, lead to paper indebtedness. Subsistence becomes ever-more insecure. It was conditions like these that the political praxis of Jesus came to address. It is conditions like these that are encountered in many of Jesus' parables, the best evidence we have for Jesus' political concerns.

Jesus surely participated in the John-the-Baptizer movement for awhile, just how long cannot be said. Without a doubt, Jesus was baptized by John. Yet, the gospels indicate an uneasy relationship between Jesus and the Baptist Movement. I argue that Jesus rejected John's vision of a Judgmental God and end-of-the world expectation in favor of living in the midst of normal social relations. Jesus' God was Compassionate and Merciful by contrast. Peasant theology, and Jesus held peasant values close to heart, is immediate and concrete.

---

3. See Hamel, *Poverty and Charity*, 39.

Jesus went back to his artisan work, traveling to where there was significant building activity—for instance, Sepphoris, Tiberias, Capernaum, Jerusalem, Caesarea Philippi, the Decapolis cities, the Phoenician coastlands. The gospels show this travel as a "religious ministry," but this is a retrojection. On those travels, Jesus showed himself to be socially gregarious and an excellent networker (again, the parables attest this). He began to "broker" between the haves and the have-nots. We see this praxis mirrored in stories such as the healing of Jairus's daughter in Mark 5 or Luke's account of Jesus at dinner with Simon the Pharisee and the woman of the city in Luke 7. Jesus' self-understanding comes to embrace a notion that brokering the Power of God heals and redistributes the necessities of life. Jesus apparently tied this praxis or brokering activity to meal settings and tables, and associated the liberation story of Israel with this activity—the Passover meal inviting all who are hungry to come and eat. He said, after all (Luke 11:20), "if by the finger of God I cast out the demons [thus alluding to the Exodus], then the Kingdom of God is in your very midst!" His political values moreover came to expression in the second table of his prayer—in the bid for daily bread, debt release, and rescue from courts that served only the creditors.

At some point, Jesus began to promote release of taxes and rents, while eating with tax collectors and those in debt (the "sinners"), under the claim that the Power (the ever-present Kingdom of God) granted rights of eminent domain over the necessary goods of the earth. Active tax-resistance expressed the effective healing and mealing that Jesus desired; the story of the so-called Dishonest Manager, held up as exemplary by Jesus, brings this clandestine activity up to the surface. This activity came to the notice of the authorities, probably through informers like Judas Iscariot, and Jesus came to be on the run. He was safe in public places, but when asked about the payment of the Roman tax, he dissembled. The early second-century Roman jurist Julius Paulus indicates the consequences for disturbing the new Roman Order, the Peace of Augustus, or *Pax Romana*: "The authors of sedition and tumult, or those who stir up the people, shall, according to their rank, either be crucified, thrown to wild beasts, or deported to an island." And even more tellingly "anyone who counterfeits gold or silver money, or washes, melts, scrapes, spoils, or adulterates any coin bearing the impression of the face of the Emperor, or refuses to accept it, . . . shall, if of superior rank, be deported to an island, and if of inferior station, be sentenced to the mines, or punished capitally. Slaves if manumitted after the crime has been perpetrated, shall be crucified."[4]

One of the earliest sayings of Jesus reckoned with the dangers of this political brokering praxis, this brokering between haves and have-nots in the name of the Power. In the saying preserved in the Sayings Source Q, which otherwise never mentions Jesus' death, we see the Crux of Jesus' political praxis: Jesus said, "The one who does not take one's cross and follow after me cannot be my disciple." According to Mark, Jesus was crucified between two bandits. And in the eyes of the elites, he was a thief.

Panel Two

Now we pass to the panel in Fig. 1.2. The shame of the cross has already been mentioned. In a very early hymn, preserved in Paul's Philippian letter, this memory is clearly expressed: "[Jesus] humiliated himself, staying obedient all the way to death, even death on a cross." This early Christ Hymn is of interest to us now in tracing what became of the memory of Jesus' political praxis in the name of the Power, the Kingdom of God. In short, the early Christian memory suppressed knowledge of Jesus' historical praxis, which in the eyes of the Roman Order led justly to the cross, and replaced that political memory with the dramatic story of Jesus' incarnation, his emptying or *kenōsis*, and after humiliation his exaltation to have his own eternal kingdom. Ironically, this eternal kingdom came to serve the needs of centralized agrarian power and taxation, so that the Constantinian Order of the era of the Nicene and Constantinopolitan Creeds would in one important respect betray the memory of Jesus. How did this come to pass, and how do we know?

---

4. Julius Paulus, *Opinions* 5.22.1; 5.25.1; see Scott, *The Civil Law.*

Figure 1.2: PANEL TWO

JESUS' ETERNAL KINGDOM

✠ The shame of the cross (Gal 3:13; Phil 2:8)

✠ Paul's Christ Hymn in Philippians and the later hymn in Colossians

✠ The information from Pliny the Younger and Tacitus

✠ The *nomen Christianus* as a political liability—but not the same issue as Jesus' historical politics

✠ Factors in the emergence of High Christology, Roman emperor worship and contested political loyalties

✠ The importance of Jesus' preexistence, consubstantiality with the Father, and eternal Kingdom

✠ Constantine, IHS, *in hoc signo vinces*, "in this sign [the cross in the sun] you will conquer," before the defeat of Maxentius at the Milvian Bridge; also, the CHI–RHO insignia

✠ The Nicene/Constantinople creed as an element in the political legitimation of the emerging Christian empire of Constantine, which is political betrayal of Jesus, who opposed exploitative agrarian taxation

---

It is useful to compare the Christ Hymn of Paul's day in the Philippian letter, written to a group of Christ-followers in Europe (Macedonia) and surely a reflection of ideas in Syrian Antioch if not Jerusalem, with the later Christ Hymn preserved in Colossians. I take Colossians to be an epistle written in Paul's name to address later circumstances in Asia Minor or ancient Turkey.

Christ Hymn, Philippians 2:5–11 (Europe)	Christ Hymn, Colossians 1:13–20 (Asia Minor)
Christ Jesus who, though he was ① *in the image [form] of God,* ② *did not regard "being like God" [equality with God] as something to be stolen [exploited],* but emptied himself, taking the form of a slave, being born in human likeness. And being found in human form, he humbled himself and became obedient to the point of death–even death on a cross. Therefore ③ *God also highly exalted him and gave him the name that is above every name [i.e., Kyrios],* so that at the name of Jesus every knee should bend, in heaven and on earth and under the earth, and every tongue should confess that Jesus Christ is Lord, to the glory of God the Father. (NRSV modified) ①②③ are missing in this earlier hymn (ca. 55 CE); for Paul, ① Jesus is the New Adam, who is perfectly human as God originally wanted (Gen 1:26–27; 1 Cor 15:21–22, 45–49; Rom 5:15–19; 8:29); ② who did not take the path of Adam (Gen 3:5); ③ and who consequently receives the highest honor in the New Creation. The kingdom remains God's kingdom. See also, 1 Cor 15:3–8, 20–28; Rom 1:3–4.	He has rescued us from the power of darkness and transferred us into ③ *the kingdom of his beloved Son,* in whom we have redemption, the forgiveness of sins. He is the ① *image of the invisible God, the firstborn of all creation; for in him all things in heaven and on earth were created, things visible and invisible, whether thrones or dominions or rulers or powers—all things have been created through him and for him. He himself is before all things, and in him all things hold together. for in him all things in heaven and on earth were created, things visible and invisible, whether thrones or dominions or rulers or powers—all things have been created through him and for him.* He himself is before all things, and in him all things hold together. He is the head of the body, the church; he is the beginning, the firstborn from the dead, so that he might come to have first place in everything. For ② *in him all the fullness of God was pleased to dwell,* and through him God was pleased to reconcile to himself all things, whether on earth or in heaven, by making peace through the blood of his cross. (NRSV) ①②③ developments in christology (ca. 100 CE): ① John 1:1–3; compare 1 Cor 8:6; 15:20–21; Rev 1:5; ② Col 2:9; Titus 2:13; 2 Pet 1:1; Ignatius Eph. 18:2; ③ Eph 5:5; 2 Tim 4:1, 18; 2 Pet 2:11.
Roman/Apostles' Creed (West, ca. 200 CE)—2d art.	**Nicene/Constantinopolitan Creed (East, Nicaea 325 CE & Chalcedon 451 CE)—2d art.**
① Preexistence and creative role not mentioned And in Christ Jesus His only Son, our Lord, **② No mention of consubstantiality with God the Father** Who was born from the Holy Spirit and the Virgin Mary, Who under Pontius Pilate was crucified and buried, on the third day rose again from the dead, ascended to heaven, sits at the right hand of the Father, whence He will come to judge the living and the dead **③ No mention of an eternal kingdom of Jesus**	And in one Lord Jesus Christ, ①② *the only-begotten Son of God, begotten from the Father before all ages, light from light, true God from true God, begotten not made, of one substance with the Father, through Whom all things came into existence,* Who because of us men and because of our salvation came down from heaven, and was incarnate from the Holy Spirit and the Virgin Mary and became man, and was crucified for us under Pontius Pilate, and suffered and was buried, and rose again on the third day according to the Scriptures and ascended to heaven, and sits on the right hand of the Father, and will come again with glory to judge living and dead, ③ *of Whose kingdom there will be no end*

Creed texts taken from Kelly, *Early Christian Creeds.*

These two hymns differ in at least three important respects. First, the Colossian Hymn asserts Jesus' preexistence, "the first-born of all creation" (a phrase that will cause problems for Athanasius and Nicaea) and "in him everything was created." Second, Colossians 1 speaks of "the kingdom of [God's] beloved son." Third, Colossians speaks in two separate places of the "deity that dwells in Jesus Christ bodily" (Col 1:19; 2:9). In the Philippians Hymn, no preexistence is mentioned; Jesus' exalted status is simply that of the New Adam with the "name above every name," that is, *Kyrios* or Lord; and no mention is made of Jesus' kingdom (in fact, 1 Cor 15:20–28 makes it clear that Jesus plays only a brokering role in bringing his own clients into God's eternal kingdom). Interestingly, as we will see in a moment, these three differences also are retained respectively in the European or Roman Apostles' Creed and the Asian or Nicene/Constantinopolitan Creed.

The embarrassment of Jesus' death on a Roman cross was not easily forgotten nor glossed over. The eastern Roman world well knew what Paul did, that this death was the most shameful death the Romans could devise. Not only did it shame the victim, but also the victim's family and friends. The embarrassment began to be papered over, so to speak, in the passion narratives of the New Testament. One need only think about Pilate's washing his hands and the Blood Libel in Matthew's Gospel, or of Luke's centurion declaring Jesus innocent at the foot of the cross, or of Pilate's attempt to release Jesus in the Gospel of John. The Seer John of Revelation believes that Jesus' true followers must also "witness unto death" against Rome if they are loyal to his witness. Loyalty to Jesus means disloyalty to Rome. In the early second century, Pliny the Younger famously writes to the emperor Trajan to ask what to do with Christians who meet in secret over a meal and sing hymns to Christ as to a god (*Epistles* 10.96). This suspicion of the Name also is shown in the Roman historians Suetonius and Tacitus. Tacitus especially is instructive:

> Christus, from whom the name had its origin, suffered the extreme penalty during the reign of Tiberius at the hands of one of our procurators, Pontius Pilatus, and a deadly superstition, thus checked for the moment, again broke out not only in Judaea, the first source of the evil, but also in the City, where all things hideous and

shameful from every part of the world meet and become popular.[5]

The very name Christian, *nomen Christianus*, was during the second century associated with treason. And loyalty tests, including the burning of incense to the emperor in a sacral context, are attested in the cases of the martyrs Justin and Polycarp. Yet, the *Christiani* are not mentioned as resisting taxation or advocating debt forgiveness. In fact, 1 Peter and the Pastoral Epistles urge giving honor to the authorities, including the emperor, and Rom 13:1–7 (probably inserted into Romans by the editor of Paul's letters toward the end of the first century) admonishes that the authorities be respected and taxes be paid. Also, Matt 17:27 seems to enjoin tax-payment of the *Fiscus Judaicus*, the Jerusalem temple tax that was redirected by Vespasian to the Temple of Jupiter in Rome after the Judean temple destruction in 70 CE!

Our story continues in conjunction with the emergence of Christian creeds. One remarkable development that goes with the political theme has already been adumbrated. Jesus' concern had to do with the Kingdom of God. As Rudolf Bultmann once remarked, after Jesus' lifetime, the Proclaimer became the Proclaimed.[6] Paul, the Sayings Source Q, and Mark enshrine the earliest understandings of this proclamation. It is entwined with the interpretive apparatus of Judean eschatology—Jesus was understood as the Messiah in service of the arrival of God's final rule on earth. His historical activity was portrayed, as argued by recent Jesus scholarship, as a movement to renew Israel. He calls the Twelve, he is conscious of being the Messiah, he goes to his death in service of the New Age that is coming. The thought worlds of Paul, Q, and Mark (our earliest witnesses to these developments) are all shaped by Judean eschatology, and Jesus in all three significantly will return to judge and claim his own. None of these three mentions where Jesus might have been before his appearance on the historical stage.

This is the predominant mode of interpreting Jesus' theological significance up until the Judean-Roman war of 66–70 CE. A different mode comes into view as voices from the Greco-Roman cities,

---

5. Tacitus, *Annals* 15.44.4.

6. Bultmann, *Theology of the New Testament*, 1:33.

notably those standing in the Pauline and Johannine traditions, begin to shape understandings of Jesus in ways more comprehensible to Gentiles or non-Judeans. Notable here will be the clear emergence of the belief that Jesus as God's Son is his only begotten Son, and that Jesus is not merely a human Messiah but now one who shares in the very nature of God and then becomes incarnate.

This development is most evident in the first-century New Testament materials that were shaped in Roman Asia and ancient Turkey. And it is carried in the next few centuries by those—Ignatius, Justin, Irenaeus—whose thought about Jesus was significantly shaped by Christianity in Roman Asia. For it is precisely in Roman Asia, around 100 CE, that the Colossian letter and the Gospel of John assert Jesus' preexistence, his role in creation, and his unique status as God's only-begotten Son. Jerome Neyrey has argued that "divinity" in the mind of first-century Christians involved not only the final power to judge the world, but also the primal power to create the world.[7] In this sense, then, the thought world of the Seer John in Revelation is just making the transition, which is fairly complete in Colossians and John. In Revelation, Jesus' preexistence is not overtly stated, although he is the Alpha and the Omega, but his role in world judgment is clear in chapters 19–20. Moreover, in the hymns sung to God in Revelation 4, God's creative powers are directly mentioned: "Worthy you are, our Lord and God, to receive glory and honor and power, for you did create all things, and by your will they existed and were created" (Rev 4:11).

How, then, did this preexistent creative power come to be associated with Jesus in his post-Easter existence? How did he move from being Paul's New Adam and Lord in the New Creation (the Philippians Christ Hymn) to Jesus Christ the Creator, embodying deity, with his own Eternal Kingdom (the Colossians Christ Hymn)? And how did this play out in the Christian tradition for several centuries until the Constantinian developments? And, to ask the Lutheran question, what do these two kingdoms mean for us?

There are at least two important things to see in the Second Panel before turning our attention finally to the Center Panel. The first important thing is the relationship between Roman imperial

---

7. Neyrey, "My Lord and My God"; and Neyrey, *Render to God*.

worship, which was very prominent in the cities of Roman Asia, and the development of High Christology; the second important thing to note is the resistance of the early Christian creeds to the deification of Jesus!

While the *mos maiorum* or "moral sense" of traditional Roman society rejected kingship and divine honors for human rulers, Caesar Augustus was quite happy to assume his imperial role as "first among equals" (*primus inter pares*) among the Roman elites, and he was equally happy to allow worship of Rome and even the emperor in the East. An inscription from Priene in Roman Asia (about 9 BCE) famously states:

> Since Providence, which has ordered all things and is deeply interested in our life, has set in most perfect order by giving us Augustus, whom she filled with virtue that he might benefit humankind, sending him as a savior, both for us and for our descendants, that he might end war and arrange all things, and since he, Caesar, by his appearance (excelled even our anticipations), surpassing all previous benefactors, and not even leaving to posterity any hope of surpassing what he has done, and since the birthday of the god Augustus was the beginning of the good tidings for the world that came by reason of him . . .[8]

Caesar's achievements merit him these honors, but it was a close next step for Greeks to sing hymns to him as to a god. We know from inscriptions that the worship of Rome and Caesar was conducted in Pergamum, and in many Asian associations, and that there was a special Choir of the West, that is, West Roman Asia, devoted to the singing of these hymns. Caesar even provided resources to support these choirs, since they were good expressions of loyalty. Religion served imperial politics quite well, thank you!

The hymns we see in Revelation take on added significance in the light of the emperor cult, since the hymns express a contest of loyalties and patrons. It was precisely in this context that the Colossians Christ Hymn was formulated, as well as the familiar words of John 1, "In the beginning was the Word, and the Word was with God, and God was the Word . . . Through the Word all things came to be

8. Translation in Finn.

. . . and the Word became flesh." Indeed, the Colossian household duties make no mention of respect for political authorities, as do 1 Peter and 1 Timothy. And it is in Col 2:15 that we find the politically resonant statement, Christ "having disarmed the powers and the authorities boldly showed them up, having led them in triumph." High Christology, in other words, was born out of Christian worship in a context of contested political loyalties.

The early Christian creeds, however, show that High Christology was not easily adopted. Partly, this may have been because of the second-century development of the view that Jesus had only seemed to be human, or because of efforts to deny that the creator God was the father of Jesus. But these ideas took Jesus even farther away from the imperial political arena. In the catholic camp, the Syro-Palestinian, North African, and Roman creeds for several centuries resisted Colossians on expressing the three major differences—the second article of the Roman Creed (the basis of the Apostles' Creed) is instructive:

> [I believe] in Christ Jesus His only Son, our Lord, Who was born from the Holy Spirit and the Virgin Mary, Who under Pontius Pilate was crucified and buried, on the third day rose again from the dead, ascended to heaven, sits at the right hand of the Father, whence He will come to judge the living and the dead . . .[9]

Notice that there is no assertion of Jesus' preexistence, no elaboration of his sharing in God's divine substance, and no eternal kingdom. Arius, famously, understood Jesus as created Word or Logos, but said with old tradition, "There was a time when he was not." The time was right for a political solution!

With the appearance of the Nicene Creed in 325 CE, we see creative preexistence and the elaboration of Jesus' relationship to God as of one substance with the Father. With the appearance a little over a century later at Chalcedon, the final piece is added: Jesus "sits on the right hand of the Father, and will come again with glory to judge living and dead, of Whose kingdom there will be no end."[10]

These creedal assertions, sponsored by imperial power, were dramatic innovations in the catholic tradition of Christian belief

---

9. Kelly, *Early Christian Creeds*, 102.

10. Ibid., 216, 297.

about Jesus. From the political point of view, they were developments especially welcomed by imperial power. For it was Constantine, after all, the convener of Nicaea, who had seen the cross in the sky before defeating Maxentius at the Milvian Bridge. IHS, the abbreviation for Jesus in Greek or in Latin *in hoc signo*, "in this sign you will conquer" (Eusebius, *Life of Constantine* 1.28). And it was Constantine who legalized Christianity as a bulwark to his new empire centered in Constantinople. And it was Constantine who could see his own alliance with the only begotten Son as divine legitimation, having neglected Jesus' humble historical station and political praxis to broker the Power on behalf of the tax collectors and sinners. This was the ultimate political betrayal of Jesus—the one who had opposed debt and taxation in the name of the Power was now coopted to legitimate that taxation in an emerging Christian Empire. Christ the King, Christus Rex, Christos Pantocrator, reigns from the cross, at the right hand of the emperor supreme!

Center Panel

Above the altar in the church, in the library or galleries of the university or museum, we turn our attention to the Center Panel of our triptych (Fig. 1.3). There we see two emblems—a table and a figure with raised hands (the *Orans* or *Orante*). "Do this in remembrance of me," he said. As he sat at his final table, in truth if not in historical actuality, he identified wholly with the Passover bread and the wine. These were his central meaning and purpose, as he had come to understand them, and perhaps with the guests around the table he invoked the Power:

> Blessed are you, O Lord our God, King of the Universe,
> provider of the bread and the fruit of the vine.

Jesus asked once again in his prayer that daily bread become secure, that debts be released, that defaults on mortgages not end up in court. As he often said, in line with the opening words of the Passover meal,

> This is the bread of poverty
> which our ancestors ate in the land of Egypt;

let all who are hungry enter and eat;

this year we are in exile,

next year may we be free.[11]

The Q scribes had remembered his typical statements in their opening inscription of his words: How honorable are you poor; how honorable are the hungry; how honorable are those who mourn—for the Power is at hand to heal and provide.

Fig. 1.3: CENTER PANEL

Byzantine altar base at Dominus Flevit

http://198.62.75.4/www1/ofm/sbf/escurs/Ger/13altareBig.jpg

Orante (with Greek word "Peace")

http://www.salomoni.it/davide/theology/blog/2006/10/
animals-in-synoptics.html

Give us today our daily bread,

Release our debts, as we release those in debt to us,

And deliver us from the evil creditor's court.

11. Glatzer translation of the opening words of the Passover Seder.

In the center of the Christian memory, therefore, is not an altar but a table, not a sacrifice but a meal, not a political apotheosis but a compassionate plea and worldly engagement. In that Center Panel, we are called continuously to transform the altar into a table. At the table is the real presence of the Power Jesus brokered between the haves and the have-nots. His politics were about redistribution, not property; about reciprocal sharing, not Mammon; and finally about the fullness of life here and now.

> In truth, Jesus' political aims remain to be contemplated and taken seriously. They are not confined to first-century Galilee, nor need they be relegated to some dustbin of history. They were a response to the Power, and the same Power still stands behind and energizes all things. Jesus' total identification with the Power led to his absorption into it as God's only begotten. In the Christian tradition and church, the Power is seen as through a glass darkly. It is there, present, where the Gospel is preached and the sacraments are administered. But the Power is not confined to church, nor need it abolish modern politics or the separation of church and state. It challenges to the core, however, the plutocrats of a new age of Mammon, whose politics and commerce will be far more destructive and disastrous for global affairs than the Roman Peace. The truth still stands, as it did for Jesus by the lakeside, that you cannot serve God and Mammon. There is still desperate need for redressing the gross inequities of power and wealth across the globe, for a shared vision of a humane future. For the political elites of this time, in Christian lands, who have not closed their hearts and minds to words of the Galilean, the political aims of Jesus may once again inspire creative ways of healing and feasting in the presence of the beneficent Power.[12]

12. Oakman, *The Political Aims of Jesus*, 138.

CHAPTER 2

Jesus and Agrarian Palestine: The Factor of Debt

Chronic indebtedness ordinarily meant catastrophe for ancient peasantries. Indebtedness mortgaged the annual agricultural production, deprived the producer of control over productive decisions, and endangered the producer's food security. This chapter explores with the help of conceptual models and comparative data the social dynamics of debt in early Roman Palestine. In turn, it will be argued that Jesus' historical activity expressed a deep concern for contemporaries whose lives had been mortgaged by perennial indebtedness.

The value of utilizing conceptual models in the study of the past is that of allowing the known to illuminate the unknown, of testing how things were on the basis of how the modern researcher conceives they might have been. Models make explicit the assumptions and judgments of the student and help to trace the connections between bits of evidence in the effort to eliminate less adequate interpretations. Models also help to build the big picture, much like a mosaic. The study of history in this way becomes a history of interpretive "successive approximations."[1]

In a similar way, comparative study lends precision and focus to the kinds of questions the historian brings to this task. Employment

1. The work of Carney, *Shape of the Past,* has broadly influenced this approach. This chapter originally appeared as an SBL seminar paper in 1985, thus ante-dating my published dissertation *Jesus and the Economic Questions of His Day.* Minor updating and revisions have been done for this version.

of social-scientific studies in various ways can contribute to a more adequate interpretation of particular aspects of the past.

Preliminary Considerations about Debt in Antiquity

Many of Jesus' fellow Israelites labored under a crushing load of indebtedness (including taxes, tributes, tithes and religious dues, land rents, as well as "borrowed money").[2] The problem of debt exacerbated the quality of relations between the owning class of agrarian, first-century Palestine and those who were forced for one reason or another into tenancy or wage labor. Debt was one of the major mechanisms whereby the rich kept getting richer and the poor, poorer. Through debt, ownership of the patrimonial land of the Judean and Galilean peasantry could be, and was, wrested from them. The "rights" of the creditor were only a manifestation of an insensitive egoism that demanded security and securities to the detriment of the well-being of all.

Debt was always a formal expression of relations of dependency and (perhaps irredeemable) obligation. The ideals of reciprocity and social equality in the Graeco-Roman and Israelite traditions encouraged hopes for more "horizontal" relations in society, but more often than not imbalances of power and wealth led in fact to "vertical" relations of dominance and subjection. For this reason, "release from debts" and "redistribution of land" were standard demands in the revolutionary movements of antiquity.[3]

For the Greeks, the most fundamental debt was that to one's parents. So Plato writes:

> Next comes the honour of living parents, to whom, as is meet, we have to pay the first and greatest and oldest of all debts, considering that all which a man has belongs to those who gave him birth and brought him up . . .[4]

Aristotle also speaks of this primal debt:

---

2. Von Kippenberg, *Religion und Klassenbildung*; Theissen, *Sociology*; Freyne, *Galilee from Alexander the Great to Hadrian*.

3. De Ste. Croix, *Class Struggle*, 298, 307, 357, 609 n. 55, and 611 n. 14.

4. Plato, *Laws* 4.717 (Jowett); for other Greek material, see Hauck, "Ὀφείλω."

This is why it would not seem open to a man to disown his father (though a father may disown his son); being in debt, he should repay, but there is nothing by doing which a son will have done the equivalent of what he has received, so that he is always in debt.[5]

Aristotle further considers in the *Ethics* how essential reciprocity is to friendship, and whether it is better to return a favor (and thus stay out of debt), or to accept such as something that cannot be paid.[6]

The socio-political aspect of debt is expressed well by Thucydides in the mouth of Pericles:

In generosity we [sc. the Athenians] are equally singular, acquiring our friends by conferring, not by receiving, favours. Yet, of course, the doer of the favour is the firmer friend of the two, in order by continued kindness to keep the recipient in his debt; while the debtor feels less keenly from the very consciousness that the return he makes will be a payment, not a free gift.[7]

On the Roman side, the vertical and political realities of debt were frequently evident. Cicero criticizes Sulla and Caesar for having expropriated property in order to bestow (politically useful) benefits on others. For Cicero, "liberality" in this sense is not just.[8] Plutarch tells how Caesar ran up huge debts for the purpose of sustaining his own political position and agenda.[9]

It is in this context that the whole subject of clientage needs to be mentioned. In the late republic and early empire, political networks were established, maintained, or destroyed by the bestowing of political favors, loans of money, or other social goods. This is well illustrated, for instance, in the affairs of Roman client aristocrats like the Herods. To give just a few examples, Antipater quickly won Caesar's friendship in Egypt by supplying a small army to support the actions of Mithridates. This gained high honors for Antipater

5. Artistotle, *Nicomachean Ethics* 8.14, 1163b19 (Ross).

6. Ibid., 8.13, 1162a34–1163a23; 9.2, 1165a3 respectively.

7. Thucydides, *Peloponnesian War* 2.40.2 (Crawley–Feetham).

8. Cicero, *De officiis* 1.43; 2.84.

9. Plutarch, *Caesar* 5. Finley discusses this kind of politics in *Ancient Economy*, 53–54, 143, and 187 nn. 47, 55.

(that is, Caesar cancelled his obligation to Antipater and made him a client).[10] Herod was unable to hide the support he had given to Antony when he presented himself to Octavian at Rhodes.[11] With his usual boldness, Herod made a point of his former loyalty to Antony as a potential asset to the new leader. To this appeal, Octavian was favorably inclined: "So staunch a champion of the claims of friendship deserves to be ruler over many subjects."[12]

If debt was at times the bond of friendship or the cement of political relations in Graeco-Roman antiquity, for "little people" it was more often than not brutal compulsion and oppression.

> The real difference between rich and poor people was in terms of security. Richer people had a wide margin of safety because of times of trouble they could resort to lower-quality meats, barley, and more legumes. They had possession of, or access to, larger and militarily safer stores. The main characteristic of the poor, on the contrary, was to be so dependent on barley, legumes (of the less desirable quality), and wild plants that when any catastrophe struck, death was at the door. The Midrash on Lamentations puts it tersely: "While the fat one becomes lean, the lean one is dead."[13]

> Debt was a permanent feature of the economic structure . . . From the point of view of the landowner, the existence of debt was a sign that the correct degree of extraction was being applied to his tenants.[14]

The abolition of debt was frequently encountered as a revolutionary slogan of the disenfranchised, usually accompanied by a demand for the redistribution of land.[15]

---

10. Josephus, *War* 1.187, 193–94, and cf. 199.

11. Ibid., 1.386ff.

12. Ibid., 1.391 (Thackeray, LCL).

13. Hamel, *Poverty and Charity*, 55.

14. Ibid., 156–57.

15. See Rostovtzeff, *SEHRE*, ch. 1; also, de Ste. Croix, *Class Struggle*, 298, 608–9 n. 55 (citing references to Aristotle, Plato, Plutarch, and others); Austin and Vidal-Naquet, *Economic and Social History of Ancient Greece*, have a good discussion of Greek developments down to the fourth century and translations

In the century and a half immediately preceding the birth of Jesus, the cases of Tiberius Gracchus, Aristonicus, and Lucullus, to name just three, give evidence of attempts to reverse or escape altogether Rome's imperialistic and exploitative agrarian policies, as well as evidence of the socially disruptive effects of debt. Tiberius, witnessing the decline of a Roman peasantry long burdened by the Punic wars and many of whose lands were in the hands of the wealthy, passed an agrarian law designed to restore expropriated lands to their former owners.[16] Tiberius was murdered. His aims were carried forward without ultimate success by his brother Gaius. The social order of Rome became dominated, again as of old, by a landed aristocracy.

Almost contemporaneously with the death of Tiberius (133 BCE), Attalus III bequeathed his kingdom to Rome. Before a final settlement could take place, a great "slave" revolt erupted under the leadership of Aristonicus (132–129 BCE).[17] This revolt, according to Strabo and Diodorus Siculus, had a manifestly utopian aim—the foundation of an egalitarian state. The Hellenistic kingdoms of Asia Minor had exploited its agricultural peoples to the hilt. Rome could be expected to follow similar policies, as was evident to the insurgents from events in Greece. The insurgents had nothing to lose and everything to gain by revolt.

Plutarch makes the agrarian aspect of this revolt plain by connecting the aims of both Aristonicus and Tiberius Gracchus with the Stoic philosopher Blossius: Freedom was only guaranteed by equalitarian arrangements in property.[18] A Pergamene inscription (*OGIS* 338) indicates that a belated attempt was made to co-opt the insurrection by offering elevated status to the slaves involved. Though the

---

of several important passages; Brunt, *Social Conflicts*, 74ff, treats agrarian problems in the late republic.

16. Plutarch, *Tiberius Gracchus* 13; cf. Brunt, *Social Conflicts* 78–80.

17. On the social breadth of this revolt, including not only slaves but also bondmen and the urban proletariat, see Rostovtzeff, *SEHHW*, 2:757, 807–11.

18. The revolutionary actions of Mithridates several decades later were apparently modeled after those of Aristonicus, which allows more precise inference about their nature. They included remission of debts and taxes, as well as promises of land redistribution: Rostovtzeff, *SEHHW*, 2:938, 943. In addition to Rostovtzeff, Dickey, "Some Economic and Social Conditions," 396–98. Also, Tarn and Griffith, *Hellenistic Civilization*, 40–41, 125.

insurrection eventually was crushed, the initial success of Aristonicus shows how powerful the hope for freedom could be for enslaved or indebted people. Several decades later, the lower classes of Asia Minor were still ready to risk all by supporting Mithridates.

After the defeat of Mithridates, the Roman general Lucullus found the population of Asia in terrible straits because of debts owed to Roman tax collectors. The fears of the movement associated with the name of Aristonicus were realized! Lucullus opposed the interests of these "capitalists" and implemented measures to alleviate the sufferings of the province: (a) Interest was lowered to 12 percent per year, (b) interest in arrears was remitted, and (c) creditors could take annually no more than one-fourth of a debtor's income.[19] Plutarch says that these measures were successful in alleviating the crisis, but within a few short years the tax collectors and the evils associated with them were back.[20]

In the Graeco-Roman world, then, debt and related agrarian problems played a crucial role in historical developments. The same can be said on the Judean side. A long biblical tradition recognized and attempted to limit, if not completely eradicate, the disruptive socio-economic effects of debt. Prescriptions or problems related to debt are mentioned in all of the major portions of the Old Testament: Legislative (Exod 22:25–27; Leviticus 25; Deuteronomy 15; 23:19–20), prophetic (Isa 5:8; Hab 2:6), historical (1 Sam 22:2; 2 Kgs 4:1; Neh 5:1–5), and wisdom writings (Prov 22:7). The tradition uniformly opposes usury and the permanent transfer of real property (Exod 22:25; Lev 25:13; Deut 15:2).

The basic presupposition for the biblical view of debt was the equality, with various qualifications, of each member of Israel before Yahweh. This meant equality of access to the goods of life as well. Hence, the vociferous opposition in the tradition to disruptions of the social order from economic causes. The emergence of the Israelite monarchy and the concomitant social stratification gave fuel to the tradition of protest and legislation.[21] The interesting post-exilic

19. See the discussion of Plutarch, *Lucullus* 20.23 in Rostovtzeff, *SEHHW*, 2:953–55.

20. Rostovtzeff, *SEHHW*, 2:965.

21. See the article of Brueggemann, "Trajectories."

episode recorded in Nehemiah 5 gives explicit detail about how the tradition might be actualized to counter agrarian problems.

Debt and a General Model of Social Stratification in Early Roman Palestine

Almost two hundred years before Jesus' appearance on the historical stage, the early Hasmonean epoch seemed to some like a return to the glorious days of Israel (1 Macc 14:4–15). The internal political struggles and agrarian unrest under Jannaeus effectively destroyed this illusion.[22] The exorbitant exactions and suffering accompanying the Roman civil wars, the fratricidal strife of the factions of Hyrcanus and Aristobulus, the rise of Antipater and Herod—all confirmed the uncertain political status of the Judean commonwealth and a new order of economic exploitation. Although peace came with Augustus, Palestine was unquestionably an occupied country. A legacy of social disruption and hardship remained. Was this situation further exacerbated by debt?

In looking at the issue of debt in the first half of the first century CE, what actual evidence is available for assessing its historical importance? For the purposes of this essay, a distinction needs to be kept in mind between the situation in Judea and that in Galilee. Furthermore, direct and particular evidence concerning debt must be distinguished from indirect general evidence that, though it cannot prove, seems to point to the existence of a debt problem. Students of this period must appeal to both types of evidence.

Two pieces of direct evidence for a debt problem in Judea are offered here.[23] First, Josephus tells us that one of the initial actions of

22. On the agrarian aspect of this struggle, see the discussion in Applebaum, "Economic Life in Palestine," 635.

23. For a slightly different perspective, see the excellent article by Goodman, "The First Jewish Revolt." Though I had not seen this article before the first draft of this text was finished, I was pleased to note the convergence of our thinking on the direct evidence. Goodman appeals to evidence of (a) the flouting of usury laws, (b) the "προζβυλ," and (c) the burning of the archives. I was also pleased to discover at the end of Goodman's article (p. 427) a different kind of model for the dynamics of debt in Judea. In subsequent revisions of this essay, Goodman's work has encouraged me to try to distinguish more clearly the debt situation in Galilee.

the Judean insurgents in the war was the burning of the office where debt records were kept. A quotation of this passage is instructive:

> [The rebels] next carried their combustibles to the public archives, eager to destroy the money-lenders' bonds and to prevent the recovery of debts, in order to win over a host of grateful debtors and to cause a rising of the poor against the rich.[24]

Josephus records another such incident at Antioch, undertaken by people under pressure from debt (*War* 7.61).[25] The motive given by Josephus for the action of the Jerusalem insurgents parallels that of Simon ben Giora, who somewhat later offered liberation to slaves so they would support his cause (*War* 4.508). These recall similar revolutionary actions taken by Aristonicus in the late second century BCE (see above).

Following the notice just quoted, Josephus refers to the archives or record office as the "nerves" or "sinews" (*neura*) of the city. In another place, Josephus uses this same expression to refer to stockpiles of food that the competing factions were burning up to their own destruction in the besieged city (*War* 5.24). The record office, then, was seen by this former aristocrat of Jerusalem as necessary for the very sustenance of the city. Debts assure the dominance of the city over the countryside supporting it (cf. *Life* 38).

The second piece of evidence here offered is the Mishnah's narrative concerning Hillel's *prozbul*:

> A *prozbul* is not cancelled [sc. in the sabbatical year]. This is one of the things which Hillel the Elder instituted; when he saw that the people refrained from giving loans to one another and transgressed what was written in the Law, "Take heed unto thyself lest there be a base thought in thy heart, etc.," Hillel established the *prozbul*.[26]

According to *m. Giṭ.* 4:3 and *b. Giṭ.* 36a (etc.), Hillel implemented through the *prozbul* a humanitarian judicial proceeding to insure the availability of loans at the end of the sabbatical cycle. The talmudic

24. *War* 2.427 (Thackeray, LCL).
25. Cf. the discussion in Brunt, "Josephus on Social Conflicts," 151.
26. *M. Sheb.* 10:3 (Blackman); the Scripture quoted is Deut 15:9.

tradition uniformly identifies the "prozbol" (a) as a formulaic statement (*m. Sheb.* 10:4), (b) made before a court, that (c) circumvents
the usual cancellation of a debt in the sabbatical year.[27]

A number of points need to be discussed with regard to the
tradition. To start with, the Hebrew text is not pointed *prozbul*,
but rather *perôzbôl*. This philological detail does not support the
usual interpretation of the word, as meaning "to the council" (i.e.
prosboulē). Hans von Kippenberg, following Ludwig Blau, has argued
that behind the Hebrew word lies the Greek *prosbolē*, a word encountered in Hellenistic legal documents. The Greek word refers to the act
of distraining on the property of a defaulting debtor and disposing of
it through auction.[28] Mishnah *Sheb.* 10:6 supports such an interpretation of the *prozbol*: According to this passage, a *prozbol* can be written only on immovable property (primarily land and houses).

The Talmud mentions other types of debt documents, and it
is useful to try to distinguish them from the *prozbol*. Mishnah *Sheb.*
10:1 speaks of loans made with or without a "bond." Both types of
loan are cancelled during the sabbatical year. In apparent contradic-
tion to this, *m. Sheb.* 10:2 says that loans given on pledge or bonds
delivered to the court are not cancelled. In these passages, the bond
stands in contradistinction to pledges and perhaps simple verbal
agreements. The pledge and the third-party surety were older means
of guaranteeing repayment of a loan.[29]

Mishnah *Sheb.* 10:5, in which "document," "bond" (*shaṭar*) is
qualified by the noun "debt," "indebtedness" (*ḥôb*), suggests that such
documents simply record a debt and the terms of repayment. The

27. The following material in the Mishnah refers to the *prozbol*: *m. Peʾah*
3:6; *m. Sheb.* 10:3–7; *m. M. Qaṭ.* 3:3; *m. Ketub.* 9:9; *m. Giṭ.* 4:3; and the doublet
m. ʿUq. 3:10. See also other tannaitic traditions in the Talmuds and Tosephta.
The difficulty of interpreting this material is here acknowledged. The traditions
were written down in final form long after their origin. The point at issue in
many discussions is obscure and at times perhaps idealistic. Furthermore, the
Mishnah was not written to give the kind of information we are asking about.

28. See *prosbolē* in LSJ, 1504. The meaning of the word is illustrated, for
instance, in Ptolemy II's instructions to the *oikonomos* of Syria and Phoenicia,
ET in Bagnall and Derow, *Greek Historical Documents*, 96.

29. See Barrois, "Debt, Debtor," 809; Prov 6:1; 11:15; 17:18; 20:16; and 22:26
suggest why the wealthy may not have wanted to stand surety for impoverished
Judean peasants.

bond represents perhaps the emergence of an impersonal system of contractual or written guaranties in place of the traditional securities. Furthermore, the bond, like the *prozbol,* is not necessarily cancelled in the sabbatical year. The reference in *m. Sheb.* 10:2 to bonds conveyed to the court suggests delinquent loans that were due prior to the onset of the sabbatical year. The debts are still due.

It has been thought that the *prozbol* was simply a clause added to a debt document, to allow the debt to be collected in the sabbatical year (and perhaps stipulate that it is secured by real estate via a mortgage or lien). Von Kippenberg thinks that this interpretation is mistaken, because it adopts uncritically the later rabbinic view of the *prozbol.* He points out that a debt contract recovered from Wadi Murabbaʿat, Mur 18 (54–55 CE), does not contain any formula like the *prozbol.*[30] Mishnah *Sheb.* 10:4, however, does seem to lend support to the "clause interpretation." It states that the purpose of the *prozbol* is to ensure "that every debt due me I may collect whensoever I desire." This formula (especially "whensoever") could conceivably refer to the waiving of the sabbatical year forgiveness, but it can also be understood to refer to an aspect of the just-mentioned Hellenistic procedure of attaching land. The phrase "whensoever I desire" then points to the significant amount of extra-judicial power vested in the creditor. He can move against the debtor's property without further reference to the court.[31] This feature, not to speak of conveyance of land to cover a debt, was foreign to traditional Israelite and Judean law. For this reason, the later rabbis had a difficult time assessing the meaning of the innovation attributed to Hillel. Understandably, they made their interpretation along traditional lines.[32] Some authentic

---

30. Von Kippenberg, *Religion und Klassenbildung,* 139 attributes such a view to Dietrich Correns (*Schebiit*) in the latter's commentary on *m. Shebiʿit*; cf. *b. Git.* 37b.

31. Possible evidence for this is preserved in *Num. Rab.* 19:9: A creditor hauls away a debtor's, as well as the neighbor's, granary! Cf. *b. Git.* 37a, which indicates that at a later time only the Judean high court (the Beth Din) could seize property; Nicholas, *Introduction to Roman Law,* 149–53, discusses legal procedures available to Roman creditors.

32. Von Kippenberg, *Religion und Klassenbildung,* 138–39. For evidence of rabbinic debate on the meaning of the *prozbol,* see *b. Git.* 37a; on the Murabbaʿat material, see n. 59 below.

memory of the meaning of the *prozbol* is retained nonetheless in the talmudic material.

It is interesting to note what look like post-70 CE "codicils" to the *prozbol* regulations—Rabbi Huspith permitted loan arrangements to be made on a wife's or guardian's property (*m. Sheb.* 10:6) and Rabbi Eliezer declared a beehive to be immovable property (10:7, against the Sages). These apparently expanded the scope of the law. Are we to infer that lands were mortgaged to the hilt after 70, and new securities needed to be found?

The direct evidence for first-century Galilean debt, as far as I know, is found only in the Gospels. The discussion of that material is logically deferred to the next section.

Turning now to the general, indirect considerations, three will be offered. These are in turn: (1) fiscal pressure, (2) population pressure, and (3) popular unrest in the pre-70 period.[33]

F. C. Grant, over fifty years ago, argued that two competing taxation systems—the Judean and the Roman—placed an almost intolerable burden upon the agriculturalist in the early first century.[34] This has become pretty much the standard view, even though ancient historians have not as yet achieved a comprehensive picture of Roman taxation in Palestine.[35] Gildas Hamel is less sure about this since each system probably took the other into account.[36]

Evidence in Josephus and Tacitus shows repeated requests for relief from tax burdens.[37] Almost in the same breath can be men-

33. Theissen, *Sociology*, 40, lists the following "socio-economic factors" as significant in Jesus' social context: (1) natural catastrophes, (2) over-population, (3) concentration of possessions, and (4) competing tax systems. Goodman, too, notes high taxation, increasing population, and bad harvests as potential explanations for the debt problem in Judea: "Problem of Debt," 419. He downplays all of these, however, and lays emphasis upon the great influx of wealth into Jerusalem after Pompey.

34. Grant, *Economic Background*, 89.

35. Freyne, *Galilee*, 183; Theissen, *Sociology*, 44; Jones, "Taxation in Antiquity," 151–85.

36. Hamel, *Poverty and Charity*, 143.

37. Cf. Theissen, *Sociology*, 43, who cites Josephus, *Ant.* 15.365; 16.64; 18.90; 19.299. Goodman, "The First Jewish Revolt," 419 n. 15, thinks all such statements are "ideological" and points to the wealth of Judea. However, one must remember who controlled the wealth and out of whose "pockets" the taxes were paid. Invariably the burden fell upon the lower classes—those who controlled

tioned the message of the embassy to Augustus (*War* 2.85–86) and the petitions to Archelaus (*War* 2.4). These latter expressly mention reduction of taxes and people imprisoned (for debt?). Tacitus tells us (*Annals* 2.42) that Tiberius received requests from the provinces of Syria and Judea for the reduction of tribute (tax on the ground). The Romans collected an annual ground tax, the *tributum soli*; they also collected a per capita tax. With this it is to be noted that Tiberius lengthened procuratorial tenure, in order (as Josephus, *Ant.* 18.172ff. tells us) to reduce extortionate exploitation of the subject peoples.[38]

Population pressure in Roman Palestine at the turn of the eras is easily inferred by looking at the expansion of the number of villages, towns, and cities of that time compared with other periods. One may also consider the archaeological and historical evidence for extensive and intensive farming.[39] Josephus speaks of both aspects— the number of villages and intensive farming—in his description of Galilee (*War* 3.42–43).

Along with such physical evidence, one must mention the social evidence for population pressure, namely, the numerous landless who are encountered in the sources. These were "excess" peasant children without inheritance, expropriated smallholders, and anyone who had been deprived in one way or another of access to the land. Many of these emigrated in search of better economic opportunity.[40] Such elements apparently supplied the labor pool for Herod's building projects, as well as the discontents met in the pages of Josephus as

---

the least amount of wealth. If they were pressed too far, they might "bite back." The aristocracy knew this, hence the petitions for lowering the tax burden.

38. For a thorough discussion, see Hamel, *Poverty and Charity*, 142–63; compare Theissen, *Sociology*, 42–43. Baron offers further evidence, *Social and Religious History*, 1:264 and n. 20.

39. See Monson, et al., *Student Map Manual*, comparing Maps 11–1 and 12–1. Cf. the views of Avi-Yonah, *The Holy Land*, 219–21, who places the population around 2.5 million. Hamel convincingly disputes this number in *Poverty and Charity*, 139. By considering the amount of food the country could have produced maximally, Hamel arrives at a figure of around one million people. Numbers should not, however, obscure the fact that the population had probably risen to a level near the maximum that the land would support under ancient technological and social conditions. On intensive and extensive farming, see Applebaum, *Economic Life*, 646; and Hamel, *Poverty and Charity*, 116.

40. See the material collected by Theissen, *Sociology*, 34–35, 41, on Galilean emigration and Transjordanian resettlement.

bandits or messianic pretenders.[41] Here too are to be classed beggars, orphans, tax collectors, prostitutes, hired laborers, petty artisans, and the like.[42] Applebaum has called attention to the expropriations of Judean and Galilean agriculturalists in the final years of the first century BCE that swelled the ranks of these people.[43] Lack of land led to conflict, especially in Upper Galilee and Perea, between Judean and Gentile cultivators. We also remember the hostility exhibited by the Galileans during the War toward Sepphoris and Tiberias—both with pro-Roman sentiments and at one time or another seat of the debt archives.[44] It is highly probable that other social mechanisms, like persistent indebtedness, were systematically adding to this pool of the disenfranchised.[45]

Consider the model sketched in Figure 2.1. The model is designed to show, in a general way, the pressures imposed by debt upon the lives of the lower social strata of ancient Palestine. In the lower part of the model, two continua are employed. The dependency scale marks a social continuum from a relatively independent status to a dependent status. The property scale represents an economic continuum from direct control and access to the land ("ownership") to indirect or no access to the land ("expropriation, dispossession"). The scales are oriented so that the greatest condition of dependency or lack of access to land is farthest from the upper part of the model— representing the upper social stratum.[46]

41. Ibid., 35–36.

42. See the discussions in Schottroff and Stegemann, *Jesus*, 15–28; Stegemann, *The Gospel and the Poor,* 13–21; and Stegemann and Stegemann, *The Jesus Movement*, 79–95.

43. Applebaum, *Economic Life*, 660.

44. Josephus, *Life* 38–39, 123ff, 375, 384. See Freyne's discussion of the Galileans in *Galilee*, 166.

45. Brunt thinks so too, "Josephus," 151.

46. For the notion of dependent labor, see Finley, *Ancient Economy*, 69 and passim. Also, de Ste. Croix, *Class Struggle*, 205ff.

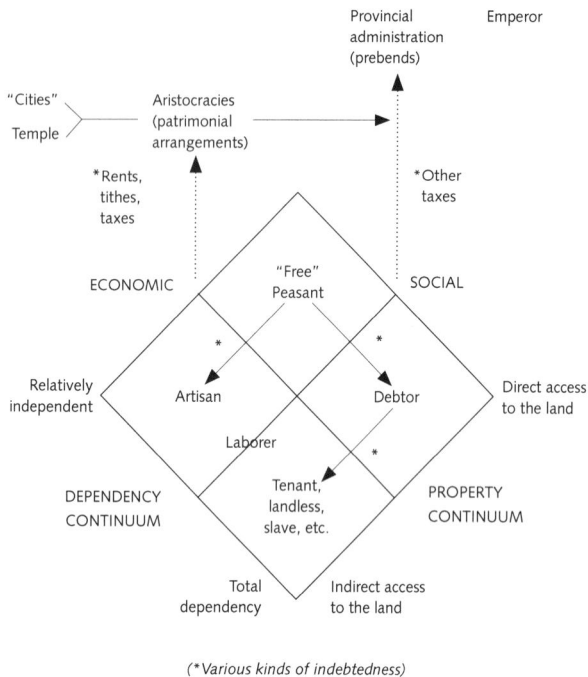

Figure 2.1: Social Dynamics of Debt in First-Century Palestine

(*Various kinds of indebtedness)

The dotted lines connecting the two major sections of the model display the flow of rents and taxes upward.[47] These place a heavy burden on the peasantry. In addition, "acts of God" contribute to the pressure toward debt and foreclosure. A variety of such factors can be mentioned here, though for lack of space they cannot be indicated in Figure 2.1. Insufficient rain or drought, insects, crop diseases, and other pestilences make their contribution. The degree to which the Palestinian economy was monetized would affect the rate of insolvency. Trade and surplus funds to loan are an important ingredient in the rise of indebtedness. Opposed to "acts of God" would be "acts of humans"—greed, speculation, and power struggles all play a role in the concentration of property, which is the reverse of the coin of

47. Cf. the diagrams in von Kippenberg, *Religion und Klassenbildung*, 92, 114, 127.

debt and insolvency. In addition, mention should be made of war, revolts, and social banditry.[48]

The top of the model indicates the oligarchic structure of Roman Palestine, as it was also articulated with the centralized state of the empire. The basic "polarity" of the top part of the model is the opposition between decentralized aristocracy and centralized ruler (with bureaucratic apparatus).[49]

The debate surrounding Grant's thesis has already been mentioned. The model suggests that not two, but three contending taxations burdened the producer in this period. In addition to the needs of the state and the old aristocracy (the high-priestly families), the needs of the new aristocracy (Herodians) and prebends for the Roman officials (prefects and procurators) must be kept in mind.[50] These may at times, as Hamel has suggested, have complemented each other. Yet one suspects that for the most part the old and new aristocracies competed for the same territory.

Debt probably was most thoroughly exploited by those aligned with Rome. This is basically a surmise, of course, but the previous discussion of the Hellenistic legal basis for expropriation of land would certainly point to such an alignment. It may also point to strong economic reasons for the secularization of the high priestly office and the upper priestly crust. In order for these to effectively compete, they would have had to adopt the methods of the new order.[51]

Bonds and pledges as guarantees for loans have already received some attention. Mishnaic laws, though mostly concerned with

48. Theissen, *Sociology*, 41; cf. *Ant.* 17.307, 355; 18.2 on Herod's possessions. Stegemann's comment is instructive (*Gospel and the Poor*, 19): "Herod the Great's expropriation of enormous stretches of farmland which were then sold to wealthy landowners . . . led to huge concentrations of land in the hands of a few . . . This in turn created great numbers of dependent tenant farmers."

49. On this polarity, see Lenski, *Power and Privilege*, 229ff. For discussions of the notions of "patrimony" and "prebend," see Max Weber, *Economy and Society*, 1:222 (prebend = benefice), 231ff.; further, Wolf, *Peasants*, 50ff.

50. See Baron, *Social and Religious History*.

51. Consider Josephus' remark about slaves of the high priests seizing produce destined for the lower orders of priests in *Ant.* 20.181, 206; see Jeremias, *Jerusalem*, 181. Consider also the role that lower orders of priests played in the Judean–Roman War (66–70 CE).

movable or immovable securities, speak also about limited periods of debt bondage.[52] Limited debt bondage is very much in the spirit of Old Testament laws forbidding interest, prohibiting the alienation of property, and protecting any necessity of life (Deut 23:19; Exod 23:26). This type of security is to be distinguished from unlimited debt slavery—a possibility under Roman law. In fact, the Roman law of debt was extremely harsh by comparison (see further the next section).[53]

As Figure 2.1 shows, "free" peasant smallholders—not, of course, free of taxes and religious dues—could become dependent upon some creditor without initially losing direct access to the land. They would remain on their ancestral plot with the legal status of "debtor," which at some point crossed over into tenancy.[54]

The model suggests the following possible scenario:[55] A bad harvest or excessive taxation, coupled with the need of the Palestinian peasant to feed his family and set aside grain for animals or the next crop, led to arrears. When this was compounded with low productivity or successive bad years, default ensued.[56] The tax collector, or a wealthy man advancing credit, might insist on securing a fiscal debt through property. The peasant, obviously, would try to secure it with the labor power of his offspring or something less valuable. Besides "legal processes," there were even dishonest machinations: *y. Ta'an.* 69a tells how the people of Beitar rejoiced over the fall of the

---

52. On this point, Goodman, "The First Jewish Revolt," 423 n. 40 follows Urbach; see *m. 'Ed.* 8:2; also, von Kippenberg, *Religion und Klassenbildung*, 143.

53. On the Roman law of debt, consult Finley, *Ancient Economy*, 40, 69; and de Ste. Croix, *Class Struggle*, 165ff.

54. See Freyne, *Galilee*, 195.

55. See a similar scenario in Freyne, *Galilee*, 195: "Indeed many tenants may have originally been owners of their own plots, but in a bad year had had to barter their land in order to pay tribute or buy grain for the following season and even feed their families."

56. Josephus, *Ant.* 18.274 is noteworthy in this connection. Applebaum, "Economic Life," 660 n. 3 gives some evidence for how this might have worked: When Israelites after the War could not pay their taxes in kind to the imperial granary in Jamnia, they were forced to borrow the next year's food. A comparative instance from modern Puerto Rico shows how debt through the "advance system" contributed there to the concentration of land ownership: See Wolf, "Hacienda System," 175–76.

wealthy in Jerusalem who had defrauded them out of their ancestral lands.[57]

The overall result of escalating debt, whether its nature was private or fiscal, was the growth of tenancy and the landless class.[58] Conversely, more and more land came under the control of fewer and fewer landowners. Of both phenomena in first-century Palestinian society, there are numerous indications.[59]

Debt in the Gospel Tradition

A number of methodological problems in dealing with the New Testament material must at least be acknowledged before proceeding. Is it appropriate to use the parables, as I am about to do, to consider Jesus in his socio-historical context? Do the parables convey direct or indirect information about social conditions in first-century Galilee? Or was Jesus' speech focused in other directions, on stock images of the Mediterranean world with little connection to actual circumstances? Was the "real world" simply a take-off point for the essential element in the parables, their alternate "narrative world"?

The interpretive stance adopted in the present chapter has two elements. In the first place, it holds that public speech in an oppressive and conflicted political situation—like that of Jesus in Roman Palestine—cannot address any serious problem in material, social, or power relations without a certain indirection or obfuscation. The parables represent Jesus' attempt to publicly express critical truths in

57. Applebaum, "Economic Life," 663 and n. 2.

58. A general view of the growth of tenancy in this period is given by Rostovtzeff, *SEHRE*, 1:99–100, 291, 344–45.

59. In addition to the previous discussion and notes: The wealthy men of the immediate post-70 period—Rabbis Tarfon, Eliezer, and Gamaliel II—did not acquire their possessions overnight. See Büchler, "Economic Conditions," 33, 36, 37. Boethus b. Zonen acquired Israelite property through default on debt: *m. B.Meṣ.* 5:3 (see ibid., 39). The loan contract from the Wadi Murabbaʿat, Mur 18, is instructive on pre-70 realities (54–55 CE). It attests to a lien on (movable?) property in case of default. Mur 22 (131 CE) documents the sale of property to cover a debt. Translations and commentary on these documents in: Benoît et al., *Les Grottes de Murabbaʿat*, 100–104, 118–21. Von Kippenberg, *Religion und Klassenbildung*, 139ff.; Koffmahn, *Doppelurkunden*, 81–89, 159–62. On the mishnaic evidence for lease of fields, see *m. B.Meṣ.* 9.

such a repressive political context. For this reason, they can always with probability be made to mean something else. This was the way Jesus protected himself. However, the basic meaning of the parables must always be assessed vis-à-vis their original audience and socio-political context.

Secondly, the hermeneutical stance of this essay stems from the recognition that, if the parables are true parables (accounts of real, one-time events), their narratives will self-evidently provide source material for social history, providing one looks for overarching themes. If the parables are similitudes (typical occurrences) or even stock images, there is nevertheless an alignment between their subject matter and the interests of Jesus, as well as a convergence with the interests of the social historian. In any case, it is believed, the parables do convey information about first-century Galilee.[60]

A further set of questions then arises: What is the nature of the concern with socioeconomic realities often evidenced in the parables? Is this concern incidental or essential for understanding the historical activity of Jesus? These questions are now taken up here in terms of the particular issue of debt.

A comparison of the Parable of the Unforgiving Slave (Matt 18:23–35) and the saying Before the Judgment (Matt 5:25/Luke 12:58) is instructive.[61] Three different situations are envisioned in which a debtor has defaulted. The two images in Matthew 18 give dramatic testimony to the realities of one Hellenistic-Roman procedure for dealing with insolvency. Both are cases of "execution against the person" of the debtor.[62] In the one instance, however, the debtor and his whole family are going into slavery for fiscal default. In the other, the debtor is simply clapped into prison for a private

---

60. This belief places me generally in the camp of the historical exegetes of the parables—Dodd, Jeremias, Perrin, and most recently Bailey. I differ from them in a direct concern with the socio-economic dimension of the parables. For the distinction between "parable" and "similitude," see Smith, *Parables*, 17. All such distinctions, as Jeremias points out in *Parables*, 20, are subsumed under the *mashal* speech form.

61. I am indebted at numerous points in this analysis to von Kippenberg, *Religion und Klassenbildung*, 141ff. De Ste. Croix has a similar analysis in *Class Struggle*, 164.

62. On this "personal execution," see especially de Ste. Croix, *Class Struggle*, 164, 240.

debt. Sherwin-White has seen here the stock image of a Hellenistic king, though he orients his discussion to the "little kings"—including the Herods—who operated as vassals of the Romans under the early empire.[63] G. E. M. de Ste. Croix too sees in the parable something that might happen in the family of Herod.[64] Perhaps we are to think specifically of Herod Antipas, who exemplified such behavior in Jesus' immediate environment in Galilee.[65]

The picture in Matt 5:25 and par. is somewhat different. Here a judicial proceeding is imminent. "Making friends" with the plaintiff thus means settling the debt out of court. This suggests a private debt is in view. If there is no settlement, the debtor is in danger of imprisonment. What is different here over against Matthew 18 is the court proceeding before imprisonment. Jeremias does not believe this is an Israelite court.[66] Sherwin-White as confidently asserts that the "judge" here is a native magistrate.[67] Von Kippenberg tries to show that imprisonment for insolvency was enforced by Israelite courts, if the debtor had no real property to offset the debt (see below).[68]

Whatever the historical reality, the court of Matt 5:25 and par. had jurisdiction over those Jesus was addressing. The legal basis for its proceedings perhaps lay in part in Hellenistic-Roman jurisprudence. While the transactions of the royal house in Matthew 18 might have seemed remote, in Matt 5:25–26 / Luke 12:58–59 the experience of Jesus' audience was directly engaged.

These three New Testament depictions suggest the model in Figure 2.2.[69] The plight of the defaulting debtor is contingent upon his landed status. If the debtor has land (assuming it has secured

---

63. Sherwin-White, *Roman Society,* 134ff.

64. De Ste. Croix, *Class Struggle,* 164.

65. Cf. the thoughts of Jeremias on Matthew 18, *Parables,* 212: "The punishment of torture was not allowed in Israel. It is again evident (see vv. 25, 30) that non-Palestinian conditions are described here, unless the parable is referring to Herod the Great, who made abundant use of torture, heedless of Jewish law— but could he have been credited with the generosity of v. 27?"

66. Jeremias, *Parables,* 180.

67. Sherwin-White, *Roman Society and Roman Law,* 133.

68. Von Kippenberg, *Religion und Klassenbildung,* 142–43; his evidence is Matthew 18; 5:25; and Josephus, *War* 2.273.

69. Though von Kippenberg does not explicitly lay out this model, all of its ingredients are present in his book: ibid., 141–142, 143.

the loan), then property is sold at auction or even transferred to the creditor to settle the debt. If the debtor does not have land, imprisonment or possibly slavery are in store.

Figure 2.2: Procedures in Case of Insolvency (after Kippenberg)

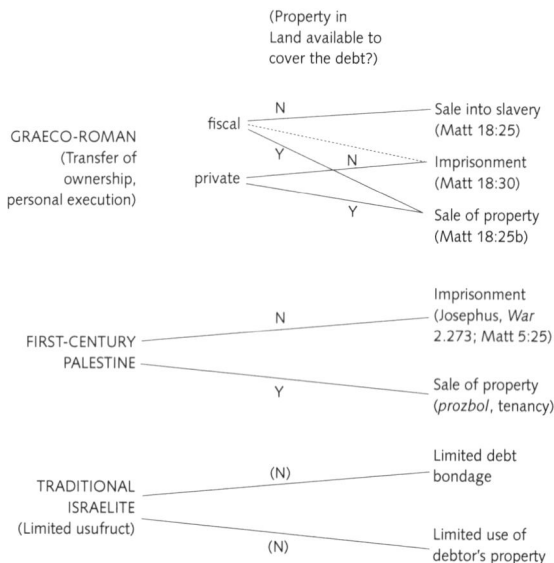

Such imprisonment probably had the purpose of forcing the debtor to cough up hidden wealth or compelling his family to redeem him. Might a public auction of a debtor's property (i.e., the *prozbol* institution) have had a similar purpose, since Israelite families would have been under pressure to "keep land in the family"? Without property, imprisonment of the debtor was more prevalent than debt bondage, both because slaves were readily and cheaply available and because there was a large labor pool of the landless. The worth of labor thereby was debased![70]

Turning to the much-discussed parable in Luke 16:1–8, a few observations about the transactions there are in order.[71] First of all,

---

70. Von Kippenberg, *Religion und Klassenbildung*; Goodman, "The First Jewish Revolt," 423 n. 40; cf. Finley, *Ancient Economy*, 70, on the worth and supply of labor.

71. Verse 9 is usually attributed to Luke (cf. the tale of Zacchaeus, Luke

the debts are paid in kind. Secondly, the size of the debts is remark-able. One hundred cors of wheat would feed 150 people for a year.[72] Similarly, the 100 *batous* (= "baths," ca. 400 liters each) amounts to a very large quantity of oil.[73] What is the nature of this debt?

Since there is nothing to indicate in the parable that the rich man is a royal figure, it is unlikely that such large debts in kind im-ply arrears in taxes. These were probably paid in money under the early empire.[74] The debtors of Luke 16 may be single tenants far in arrears on their rent.[75] The best assumption, however, would seem to be that the parable envisions a man who owns whole villages. These tenant villages, through representatives, pay a yearly produce rent on their agricultural lands. The rich man, then, sells these goods (oil and wheat would be negotiable) and/or provisions his own household. The debt in any case is a private debt. This interpretation finds sup-port in v. 4: "when I am dismissed . . . they will welcome me into their houses." By defrauding the master, the steward has made many "friends," whole villages in fact.

Of particular interest in Matt 18:23–35, Luke 16:1–8, and also in the brief story of Luke 7:41–42 is the aspect of debt forgiveness or remission. In Matthew 18 and Luke 7, a petty king or a (wealthy) money-lender supply the examples. Such things happened in the "real

---

19:1–10, where "unjust mammon" does indeed make friends). As for verse 8, it is debated whether the *kyrios* is the wealthy man of v. 1 (cf. v. 3) or Jesus. Jeremias' observation regarding Luke 18:6 seems decisive here: The Lord is Je-sus in both this parable and that of the Importune Widow. Jesus himself, then, commends the behavior of the manager who rips off his master (the steward is a slave) in order to insure his own future security.

72. This figure is derived from the following calculation: About 200 kg of grain will keep one person alive at a subsistence level for a year; on this see, Hamel, *Poverty and Charity*, 136, based upon the work of Clark and Haswell, *Economics of Subsistence Agriculture*, 58. If the Talmudic cor was around 400 liters in volume, equivalent to 11 bushels, and an average density of wheat today is around 27 kg/bu., then 100 x 11 x 27/200 = ca. 150.

73. Variant readings in D, of course, offer the smaller unit "qab," = 1/6 of the bath; compare the discussion in Jeremias, *Parables*, 181: 100 cors = yield of 100 acres. 100 baths = yield of 146 olive trees.

74. According to Rostovtzeff, *SEHRE*, 1:208–9, and as in Matthew 18; but see n. 56 above.

75. Rents were normally about 10 cors a year: *m. B. Meṣ.* 9:7. Applebaum, "Economic Life," 659.

world," according to these similitudes. Yet as we have seen, remission of debts was a revolutionary slogan in agrarian antiquity, and such tales on the lips of a Galilean prophet probably sounded subversive.

The case of Luke 16 is somewhat different. There an underling (cf. the contrary behavior of the underling in Matthew 18) reduces the indebtedness, though not entirely. The limited nature of the reduction, nonetheless, points in the same general direction as the other two stories. The betrayal of the master's trust, along with the debt transactions, suggests an abrogation of the then-current social mores of fidelity in such relations and the rigorous exaction of debt.[76]

Through the stories of Matthew 18, Luke 16, and Luke 7, Jesus offers important comment about *responses to debt forgiveness.* Matthew 18 portrays a Hellenistic monarch as a model of the mercifulness required in the act of forgiving.[77] Upon the slave's petition the king is moved with pity (v. 27) and releases the man from his obligation. This magnanimous gesture is placed in the starkest contrast by the slave's subsequent behavior. When he encounters a fellow-slave owing him a very minor sum (compared with his own previous debt), the man has the other slave thrown into debtor's prison. What callousness! This obviously is the reaction the parable was intended to elicit. The slave who had the huge debt did not appreciate the magnanimity and generosity shown to him, at least not enough to see some claim upon his own conduct. The rage of the monarch (v. 34) issues in swift punishment of this callous man.

A positive version of this parabolic point is preserved in Luke 7:41–43. In this case the response of the "forgiven" is measured by their response of love toward the merciful creditor. Response is the *tertium comparitionis* ("point of the comparison," i.e. creditor forgiving debt receives back gratitude and love) in both Matthew 18 and Luke 7. The direction of the response, whether love toward creditor or mercy toward debtors, should not be allowed to obscure the underlying point of a response that is commensurable to the experience of forgiveness or release ("love," equal generosity shown to others). "Grace" in these two stories does not come without strings attached;

---

76. Recall again the passage in Cicero, *De officiis* 2.84.

77. St. Croix, *Class Struggle,* 163.

rather forgiveness paradoxically lays an even greater burden of responsibility upon the recipients.

Response to generous forgiveness is also the desideratum of the steward's actions in Luke 16:1–8. A comparison of this parable with that of the Wicked Tenants illustrates the reversal that has taken place. There (in Mark 12:1–12) the intermediaries between owner and tenants (equivalent to Luke's steward) are abused and even murdered when they try to collect on the rent. Here the steward violates that normative order and exercises some "enlightened self-interest." The normal course for a deposed functionary of the elite is indicated in v. 3: the lot of the disenfranchised laborer or beggary. Inasmuch as these intermediaries are the enforcers of an oppressive agrarian social order, they are hated by the peasantry.

Perhaps the steward's actions are to be understood as a typical occurrence, when possible. The political astuteness of the move is, from an agrarian perspective, self-evident. Through the mechanism of releasing debtors from their obligations, the steward creates some positive alternatives for himself. Yet it cannot be overlooked that there is, from the viewpoint of the dominant culture, injustice involved (cf. v. 8, steward of unrighteousness). Why does Jesus then praise the man? Is he siding with the oppressed peasantry against the rich? To do so would not change the dominant ethos of self-sufficiency that Jesus opposes in both the landlord class and the peasantry. No, the story would seem to be aimed at the rich themselves (as Luke has well understood). What is laudable about the steward's behavior is his generosity (and with others' goods!)—a generosity certainly motivated by self-interest, but with particularly salutary effects. This is a generosity that not only mitigates oppressive circumstances, but creates the basis for a new relationship to the peasantry. To borrow terminology from Eric Wolf, a single-stranded relationship between exploitative elite and oppressed peasantry is modified by the addition of some new strands. However, the steward will no longer stand above the peasantry, but will be reduced to their level—otherwise, lower still!

Other passages in the tradition also play upon the theme of debt or debt remission. In the parable of the Talents, Matt 25:14–30/ Luke 19:11–27, the master commends slaves who have increased his wealth. This is the conventional expectation—money will be put out on loan for interest. The slave who does not utilize his master's capital to acquire more is in trouble, even though hoarding a treasure was also a socially acceptable way of handling capital.[78] In a way, this parable, like that of the Wicked Tenants (Mark 12:1–12), graphically portrays the new order of things that has come under the Romans.

The example story of the prodigal son (Luke 15:11–32) explores the problem of moral debt. The son violates conventional mores by asking for his inheritance before his father's death. In effect, the son acts as though the father is dead.[79] Yet the father's subsequent behavior violates customary mores that would consider the son also as dead. The father forgives the son's grievous social sin and restores his status. In the violation of the customary rules, Jesus sees new possibilities for life.

Of course, this concentrated attention on debt forgiveness in the Jesus tradition has not gone unnoticed by New Testament commentators, but they have rarely made out of it any material social conclusion. The suggested interpretation of these Gospel passages urges that Jesus' heart was particularly with the landless, that is, those forced for one reason or another into beggary, prostitution, tax collection, or other occupations not directly linked to working the land.[80] It may be surmised that many of these people knew the reality of indebtedness. Perhaps they had not been able to get out of debt, and so had been driven from "normal" social ties for this reason. Would such people have made no connection between their material need, and the most profound expression of the aims of the Jesus movement—the Lord's Prayer? That will be the question explored in the next chapter.

In conclusion it must be said that, if the interpretation advanced is sustainable, Jesus' activity takes on an explicitly revolutionary aspect according to the canons of antiquity. From one side, his deeds and pronouncements can be seen to have advocated the dissolution of the material mechanisms of social stratification and power. From another side, the political authorities undoubtedly would have perceived, even in the hint of a public proclamation of the abolition of

---

78. Finley, *Ancient Economy*.

79. Bailey, *Through Peasant Eyes*.

80. See the works of Schottroff and the Stegemanns cited in n. 42 above.

debt, a subversive, revolutionary agenda. Jesus did not have to advocate armed insurrection to be branded a revolutionary. In fact, he did not advocate armed insurrection. However, his vision of the liberation coming with the reign of God directly attacked a principal element of the Roman order in Palestine and attracted a following of people victimized by debt.

CHAPTER 3

The Lord's Prayer in Social Perspective

In the villages of Galilee, the Lord's Prayer
was revolutionary "wisdom" and "prophetic" teaching . . . [1]

Introduction

Much has been written about the Lord's Prayer during the modern era. It may seem as if everything has been said that could have been said. Learned disquisitions are available regarding the linguistic aspects (Greek, Aramaic, even Hebrew), the various forms of the Greek text and their relationship to Q, and the meaning of the Prayer or its individual petitions.[2]

I am centrally concerned here with the tradition history and social meaning of Jesus' Prayer. It presumes or interacts with existing scholarship, but is not intended to offer anything dramatically new related to linguistic or textual issues.[3] The canonical texts provide a

1. Duling and Perrin, *The New Testament*, 25. Duling and Perrin offer an excellent discussion of methods that have been applied in the study of the Lord's Prayer, and a valuable beginning point for further study.

2. The recent bibliography compiled by Mark Kiley includes well over 250 items; Kiley, "The Lord's Prayer and Other Prayer Texts from the Greco-Roman Era: A Bibliography."

3. The (Lord's) Prayer, for the purposes of this study, is discussed formally in terms of an address, two "tables" of two to four petitions each, and a concluding

starting point for inquiry into the tradition history. The social meaning is considered *pari passu* (in lock-step) with this history, since basic impulses in the tradition derive from conflicting social interests. The meaning for the earliest Jesus movement is parsed essentially in the light of a significant "social problem" of Jesus' day, namely, the growth of indebtedness and the swelling of the ranks of those displaced from the land because of debt. As the Prayer passed into written forms, the interests of various scribes found their way, as it were by way of glosses, into the Prayer tradition. We consider two distinct settings in life—the village and town scribal settings of earliest Q in Galilee, and the Judean-oriented scribal concerns of later Q recensions. By the time the Prayer was incorporated into canonical Matthew, Luke, and indirectly John, Judean interests had come to predominate, and basic concerns of the original Jesus movement had been reworked in systematic ways.

Basic Social Models of this Study

The employment of explicit social models provides distinctive perspectives on the "trajectory" of the Prayer from Jesus up until inclusion in the canonical gospels and later Christian traditions. Since the meaning of a prayer depends significantly upon the social system and location of the petitioner, social-scientific criticism plays a prominent role in the formulation of this essay's approach, working hypotheses, exegesis, and conclusions.[4] The meaning of the text is perceived vis-à-vis a critically reconstructed social world. The approach is thereby dialectical, and if it gives a credible and reasonable accounting of the data, and can incorporate or rule out the major alternatives, it becomes persuasive.

Recent scholarship has strongly urged that religion was imbedded in politics in Jesus' Palestine.[5] Religion and theology were

---

doxology or "ascription." Table 1 = Petitions 1–3; Table 2 = Petitions 4–7.

4. Elliott, *What Is Social-Scientific Criticism?* Regarding the relation of meaning to social system, see Malina, *The Social World of Jesus and the Gospels,* 10, 17.

5. Oakman, "The Archaeology of First-Century Galilee," orig. 220–51; Horsley, "Jesus, Itinerant Cynic or Israelite Prophet?," 80; and Malina, "'Religion' in the World of Paul."

consequently bound up with certain kinds of socio-economic interests, and it is possible to recover some of those links through our extant textual traditions. The social model that supplies the primary working assumptions of this essay, thus, begins with the consideration that *Jesus' message spoke to an immediate need in concrete terms.* As with peasants generally, Jesus had little concern for priestly mediations of the divine, or purity in the priestly sense, and was paramountly concerned with the changing of material circumstances and the institutions that controlled them.[6] He spoke out of an intense election consciousness: His experience of God was immediate and in little need of mediating institutions. This characteristic could be construed by later Judean tradents of the Jesus materials as evidence of Jesus' (messianic) authority and status. While Jesus' aims have been hotly debated, he did seem to want to articulate the meaning of Israel's core traditions, especially Moses (Passover) and the prophets (justice for the powerless), for the situation of early Roman Palestine.

Social conflicts were endemic in early Roman Palestine and are presumed as accompaniments to the activity of Jesus as well as the development of the gospel traditions. Such conflicts should not be construed naively as "Jesus (or Christians) versus the Jews." The Herods or the Judean elites in Jerusalem were often the object of popular enmity, as not only the gospels, but also Josephus and later rabbinic traditions show. The socio-political conflict which is the initial frame for understanding the Lord's Prayer is analogous to social phenomena familiar to us from the Old Testament and Second Temple Israelite writings. For instance, Micah's tirade against eighth-century Jerusalem (Mic 3:9–12) or Jeremiah's later judgment against

6. The abductive procedure here depends upon peasant studies and readings of the Jesus tradition that are justified in the subsequent pages (see Malina, "Interpretation," 259–60). For general concerns of peasant religion, see Weber, *The Sociology of Religion*, 80, 82; Wolf, *Peasants*, 101; Redfield, "The Social Organization of Tradition." Jesus of Nazareth, of course, came from the peasantry, but was not entirely limited in his own concerns to peasant horizons, as I have argued in Oakman, *Jesus and the Economic Questions of His Day*, 175–98; and Oakman, "Was Jesus a Peasant?" Jesus' "brokerage" activities, moreover, had to do with transforming, not sustaining, the socio-economic order. For a very different view of Jesus' relationship to purity, see Chilton, *The Temple of Jesus*, 133, who claims that Jesus was concerned about fulfillment of the aims of Leviticus. Jesus was still in fundamental conflict with the priestly establishment (ibid., 100–2).

the Jerusalem temple (Jer 7:8–15) provide suggestive social parallels (involving agrarian and village discontent) to the conflicts in Jesus' day. The traditions of *1 Enoch* bespeak similar social discontent in the early Hellenistic period, and the revolt of the Maccabees, beginning in the village or town of Modein, certainly had agrarian overtones (1 Macc 2:23–30). The literature of Qumran attests for the late Hellenistic and early Roman periods that Jerusalem politics, overlaid by strong religious ideology, could become quite volatile. And Josephus amply documents the "banditry" and disorder that preceded the Judean–Roman War of 66–70 CE.[7] In striking Judean analogy to the peasant prophet Jesus of Nazareth, "Jesus son of Ananus" appeared in Jerusalem in 62 or 63 CE declaring that the temple was dishonored and the people bound for disaster.[8]

The earliest scribes of the Jesus tradition, working in villages and towns of eastern Galilee, produced the first translations of Jesus' Aramaic speech into Greek. For perceptions of the original meaning of the Lord's Prayer, some appeal must be made to the Aramaic behind the (likely) Q Greek. Nevertheless, the case made in this essay about original meaning does not depend upon a precise knowledge of the original words, but only upon probable linguistic elements conjoined with social considerations.[9] There would have been a close interface, although hardly an identity, between the early Q tradents' social interests and the interests of Jesus.[10] Q was originally compiled by Galilean scribes, probably within the Herodian administration (Mark 6:14; Luke 8:3; 13:31) and not overly sympathetic to scribal interests prevalent later in the Jesus tradition (Luke 11:39–52).[11]

---

7. Material discussed at length in Horsley and J. S. Hanson, *Bandits, Prophets, and Messiahs*. See also K. C. Hanson, "Jesus and the Social Bandits."

8. Josephus, *Ant.* 6.300–305.

9. Some of these ideas and issues were first sketched much too simply, in Oakman, "Rulers' Houses, Thieves, and Usurpers."

10. I consider that Jesus was an illiterate peasant, for these reasons: 1) Jesus did not leave any written record that we know of; 2) Jesus was known through oral-speech forms (parable, aphorism); 3) generally, peasant artisans would have little opportunity for education (see Oakman, "Was Jesus a Peasant?"). Some have urged that Jesus possessed at least Torah-education, e.g., Klausner, *Jesus of Nazareth*, 234–35 (cf. 193), but this does not urge a literate education.

11. Kloppenborg, "Literary Convention" has been influential here.

Once Jesus' Prayer had assumed written form, in the language of commerce and to some extent empire, other interests would become more significant than those of the originating context. "Social-textural" considerations (to use Vernon Robbins' language) are more important at an earlier stage, "intertextural" considerations come into play at later stages.[12] Whereas an illiterate Jesus was preoccupied with the immediate and concrete, *later tradents of the Jesus tradition become more concerned with theological (christological, eschatological) abstractions or the articulation of the Jesus material with Israel's great traditions.* Also, as the Prayer was uttered within other social locations, socio-political concerns were softened (but not completely obliterated) while socio-religious concerns came more to the fore.

In general, purity concerns and apocalyptic concerns emphasizing judgment are highly correlated; as Qumran clearly shows, apocalyptic Judean interests stood within priestly and temple concerns.[13] Similarly, apocalyptic New Testament images (Mark 13; 1 Corinthians 5–6; Revelation) are filled with violence and conflict, reflecting the collision of incompatible principles. These interests are marked by a concern for God's magical intervention to rectify conditions of impurity from the standpoint of priestly sensibilities. Apocalyptic "readings" of Jesus, Jesus' aims, or Jesus material will thus have depended upon Judean scribes standing within significant temple or priestly interests (late-Q, Paul, late Mark [i.e., 11–15]).

The Canonical Texts of the Lord's Prayer

The fact that there are differing forms of the Lord's Prayer provides one of the key warrants for a tradition-critical analysis and for letting "social imagination" loose in dialectic between text and social models. It is necessary at the start to examine the textual basis for the study.

There is a modern "sociology of knowledge" issue reflected in defense of harmonistic texts, glossed understandings, or the printing

12. Robbins, *Exploring the Texture of Texts*, 40, 71.

13. The author is aware that this generalization glosses over some of the fine distinctions in recent studies, for instance Collins, "Early Jewish Apocalypticism," 287. However, even Judean apocalyptic traditions that emphasize wisdom are probably still within the orbit of priestly interests.

of both the Matthean and Lukan versions in red in Red Letter Editions. This issue is well illustrated in the history of English versions. The King James Version offers the non-specialist with perhaps the easiest access to the shape of the Lord's Prayer according to the *textus receptus*, the Greek text most common during the Middle Ages that shaped the earliest printed Greek testaments, English versions, and liturgical traditions among English-speaking Protestants. The Matthean and Lukan versions of the Prayer are printed almost identically. Missing in Luke is the final doxology; heaven and earth are reversed in Luke 11:2b; Luke's "day by day" (11:3) replaces Matthew's "this day" (6:11); Luke's "sins" (11:4a) replaces Matthew's "debts" (6:12a), and the final clause of Luke 11:4a is longer than the Matthean version (6:12b). These similarities demonstrate the well known harmonistic tendencies of *textus receptus* (in light of numerous variants in the Greek manuscript tradition of the Prayer).

Following important textual discoveries and the critical work of scholars like Tischendorf and Westcott-Hort, the English revisions in the late-nineteenth and early twentieth centuries began to incorporate more critical readings.[14] Edgar Goodspeed's *The New Testament: An American Translation* was greeted with popular indignation based in ignorance of scholarly progress in text-critical work.[15] One editorialist even suggested that the Prayer that Jesus had prayed should be left unchanged:

> Nothing stops his [Goodspeed's] devastating pen. He has even abbreviated the Lord's Prayer, a petition not so long originally but that hustling, hurrying Chicagoans could find time for it, if they ever thought of prayer. It is a petition that in its present wording has been held sacred for nearly two thousand years, for the King James translators are said to have made no changes.[16]

---

14. The English Revised Version appeared in 1881–1885 and its American counterpart in 1901: see *The Holy Bible Containing the Old and New Testaments* (1901). Westcott and Hort detailed many of the problems in their *Introduction to the New Testament in the Original Greek*.

15. Goodspeed, *The New Testament: An American Translation*.

16. Goodspeed, *As I Remember*, 176.

Goodspeed justly observed that the *English Revised Version* (1881) together with its close relative the *American Standard Version* (1901), as well as Weymouth (1903), the *Twentieth Century New Testament* (1905), and Moffatt (1913), had all printed the shortened Lord's Prayer at Luke 11:2–4.[17] The shorter Lukan text, moreover, was adopted in the Revised Standard Version, and indeed in all modern versions based upon a critical Greek text. While at least one scholar has promoted a return to something like the *textus receptus*, his arguments have not proven persuasive.[18]

Turning to the Greek text itself, eight variant readings in the Lukan prayer stem from Matthean parallels, since early copyists were often tempted to harmonize. Typical of this type of variant would be the expansion of the address in Luke: Alexandrinus and several Western manuscripts (which tend to conflate readings) have "ours in heaven." Similarly, against the majority of Greek manuscripts, Alexandrian (especially P[75]), Western, and pre-Caesarean types supply the Matthean third petition in Luke 11:2.[19]

The most interesting Lukan variant appears in 11:2: Several medieval manuscripts have for the second petition, "Let your holy spirit come upon us and cleanse us." This reading is attested in the East in the writings of Gregory of Nyssa (c. 330–395) and faintly in the West in Tertullian (c. 160–225). Perhaps the reading entered the manuscript tradition out of Montanism in the second century CE and likely in connection with baptism.[20]

The longer Matthean version of the Lord's Prayer shows no variants of the harmonistic type. The most significant variant here is the doxology or ascription—"For yours is the kingdom, and the power, and the glory, for ever"—which also appears in the *Didache* (ca. 125 CE) but not in the best manuscripts of the Alexandrian, Western, and

17. Ibid., 177.

18. Van Bruggen, "The Lord's Prayer and Textual Criticism," argues the case and is generally skeptical about modern text criticism, but Bandstra, "The Original Form of the Lord's Prayer," provides a thorough refutation.

19. The other parallels: Aorist *dos* for *didou* and *sēmeron* for *to kath hēmeran* in 11:3; *to opheilēmata* for *tas hamartias*, *hōs kai hēmeis* for *kai gar autoi*, *tois opheiletais* for *panta opheilonti hēmin*, and the insertion of *alla rhysai hēmas apo tou ponērou* in 11:4.

20. Metzger, *Textual Commentary*, 155–56.

pre-Caesarean types. (The manuscript tradition shows a number of interesting minor variations to this reading.) It would also seem to have crept into the Matthean Prayer as a gloss encouraged by liturgical usage.[21] There are numerous other minor variations between the two forms of the Prayer as well as within the manuscript tradition, but these will not be comprehensively itemized.

The manuscript tradition of the Prayer thus shows that its text was not immune to accretions or modifications. A critical Greek text, maintaining the striking differences between Matthew and Luke, must form the starting point for a consideration of the original form and meaning of the Prayer.[22]

Tradition History and the Social Contexts of the Lord's Prayer

The early tradition history of the Lord's Prayer must be reconstructed primarily through canonical New Testament materials (Q through Luke, Matthew; allusions in Paul, Mark, and John).[23] *Didache* 8 provides a point of reference for Syrian tradition after the time of Matthew, but the *Gospel of Thomas* does not allude to the prayer or seem to offer additional insight. Several earlier stages or strata can be perceived through a tradition-critical analysis of the canonical materials. The penultimate stage corresponds with the latest form of the Prayer in Q; developments from Jesus to the latest Q form are perceptible though somewhat dimly; and some proposals can be made about the form of the Prayer used by Jesus himself. We turn to an examination of these stages in reverse chronological order.

21. Ibid., 16–17; Betz, *The Sermon on the Mount*, 414–15.

22. The Nestle–Aland text, 27th edition provides this basis.

23. Brooke traces allusions more extensively in Paul and John, "The Lord's Prayer Interpreted through John and Paul." Compare the chart in Houlden, "The Lord's Prayer," 357.

Stage 3: The Latest Setting in Q

Doubt persists as to whether the Lord's Prayer pericope belonged to Q.[24] Kloppenborg accepts the Prayer as early as Q[1], since he claims it formed the core of one of the sapiential speeches. Jacobson, however, sees the Prayer as a late addition to Q (with concerns similar to the Temptation) and follows Manson in thinking that it may have been "secret teaching" reserved for the mature. Betz also urges that the Prayer entered Q rather late in two different versions, and existed only in Greek.[25]

The most persuasive reasons for seeing a Q version behind Luke and Matthew reside in the verbatim identity of Petitions 1–2 and in the word *epiousion* (usually translated as "daily"). In regard to the latter, it would be very difficult for two completely independent versions of the Prayer to convey the Aramaic by a word that turns out to be *hapax legomenon* (occurring only once) in ancient Greek. This fact seems easier to account for by means of a common Greek origin for the canonical prayers. Departures from that common form have then to be accounted for more by the evangelists' redaction than by translation, but the divergences in their language still reflect to some extent uncertainties about meaning derivative from the Prayer's earlier history.

At the latest Q stage, before the Prayer was taken up and edited by Matthew and Luke, the Q prayer had a form similar to this:[26]

---

24. Kloppenborg provides a helpful survey, *Q Parallels*, 84.

25. Kloppenborg, *Formation of Q*, 203–6; Jacobson, *The First Gospel*, 158–59; Botha, "Recent Research on the Lord's Prayer," 43. Betz, *Sermon on the Mount*, 371: "If the Lord's Prayer was part of Q, it must have become a part of it after the two versions of Q developed." He denies (375) that the Prayer ever existed in Aramaic: "no evidence suggests that the Lord's Prayer as we have it was first composed in Aramaic or Hebrew and only then translated into Greek."

26. Davies and Allison, "Excursus," 591. Duling and Perrin concur, *The New Testament*, 16.

Figure 3.1: The Lord's Prayer Form in Q

	Address	*Pater,* **Father**
Table 1	Petition 1	*hagiasthētō to onoma sou* **may your name be sanctified**
	Petition 2	*elthetō hē basileia sou* **may your kingdom come**
Table 2	Petition 4	*ton arton hēmōn ton epiousion dos hēmin sēmeron* **give us today our [meaning of** *epiousion* **uncertain] bread**
	Petition 5	*kai aphes hēmin ta opheilēmata hēmōn,* *kai gar autoi aphēkamen tōi opheilonti hēmin* **and forgive us our money debts** **as we forgive those who owe us money**
	Petition 6	*kai mē eisenegkēs hēmas eis peirasmon.* **and do not put us to the test.**

Even given a Q Lord's Prayer, the view of Jeremias that an "original Aramaic form" lies behind the Greek retains strong plausibility because of the uncertainties regarding meaning manifest in Matthew's and Luke's diverging wordings: "the Lucan version has preserved the oldest form with respect to length, but the Matthaean text is more original with regard to wording."[27] Jeremias' reasons for giving priority to the Lukan length were fourfold: 1) The strict parallelism of Matthew's version, as well as 2) Matthew's greater elaboration, suggested to Jeremias the end product of liturgical usage. Furthermore, 3) Luke's simple address "Father," in contrast to Matthew's "Our Father in heaven" (well attested in Targums and later Jewish prayer forms), seems to reflect the Aramaic address of Jesus, *'abba'*, also adopted by later Christians (Paul: Rom 8:15; Gal 4:6; *Didache* 8). Finally, 4) Jeremias noted the parallel between the Lukan version of the first two petitions of the Lord's Prayer and the *Qaddish*

27. Jeremias, *Prayers*, 93; cf. Fitzmyer, *Luke*, vol. 2, 897.

of the Jewish synagogue. The *Qaddish* begins (following Jeremias' arrangement):

> Exalted and hallowed be his great name in the world which he created according to his will. May he let his kingdom rule in your lifetime and in your days and in the lifetime of the whole house of Israel, speedily and soon. And to this, say: amen.[28]

On the other hand, Jeremias was forced to the anomalous conclusion that, in terms of the specific wording of the respective prayers, the Matthean version was at several points indicative of earlier understandings. What these observations imply is that a critical discussion of an "original Aramaic form" is still necessary, though in this task Jeremias' position requires some modifications. The changes and expansions evident between Luke and Matthew are along lines governed not only by a Semitic linguistic sensibility (Aramaic and Hebrew), but also by social interests operant in the tradition.

It is important to have some definite, even though general, ideas about the social origins of the Q recensions. Kloppenborg has provided the most satisfying proposal so far about these matters. He notes that the wisdom interests manifested in the contents and composition of Q^1 (consequently, "Wisdom Q") would be appropriate to town or village scribes, "the 'petit bourgeois' in the lower administrative sector of cities and villages. It is plain from Egyptian evidence that it is precisely within these sectors that the instructional genre was cultivated."[29] Moreover, wisdom was usually the concern of royal administrative personnel. And Q^1's metaphorical preoccupation with an "alternate kingdom" would indicate this as well.[30] It goes a step beyond Kloppenborg, though he sparks the thought, to suggest that Herod Antipas' administrative personnel around the Galilean Lake probably provided the first Q draft (as indicated by Matt 9:9?). Kloppenborg tantalizingly suggests that the transfer of the city of Tiberias

28. Jeremias, *Prayers*, 98.

29. Kloppenborg, "Literary Convention," 85. Jacobson's reservations about "wisdom" (*First Gospel*, 257) are noted. He prefers to account for Q transformations by appeals to the diachronic experiences (256) of a single group, while the proposal here assumes activity in different scribal spheres.

30. Kloppenborg, *Formation of Q*, 317–20.

to Agrippa II (54 CE), and concomitantly the royal archives back to the city of Sepphoris, left its mark in the Q tradition in the move to prophetic forms. It certainly makes sense, given that ancient recensions were frequently connected with changes in political fortunes, to connect the more heavily Judean character of Q² ("Deuteronomic Q") with the work of Sepphorean scribes.[31] These considerations would urge dating Q¹ somewhere between the late 20s and 54 CE, and Q² somewhere in the period 54–66 CE.[32]

Zahavy has lent insight into the sociology of scribalism around the time of the Judean–Roman War. In the immediate aftermath, he sees a struggle between scribes who focused their ultimate concerns and piety around the *Shema ͑* and Deuteronomy and scribes whose interests congregated in the *Amidah*. As he sees the situation:

> In the crucial transitional period after the destruction of the Temple, the *Shema ͑* emerged as the primary ritual of the scribal profession and its proponents. The Amidah . . . was a ritual sponsored mainly by the patriarchal families and their priestly adherents.[33]

Both of these scribal groups were involved in Jerusalem–Judean affairs, but Zahavy's "professional scribes" would have been less tied to Jerusalem than families associated with the temple and priesthood. Therefore, post-temple Judaism was to be (as Zahavy sees it) a compromise between these two scribal interests, attested in the combination of *Shema ͑* and *Amidah* in the synagogue service. What Zahavy's work suggests about the Q tradents, assuming similar circumstances a quarter century or so before, is this: Q¹ was the product of Herodian scribes; Q² was the product of Judean scribes whose theological commitments were expressed through the *Shema ͑*. A logical line from Q¹ to Q² and the later synoptic tradition (in strong argument with Pharisees and post-temple developments) can begin to be traced.

---

31. Coote and Coote, *Power, Politics, and the Making of the Bible*. On the Judean character of Sepphoris, see S. S. Miller, *Studies in the History and Traditions of Sepphoris*.

32. Jacobson, *First Gospel*, 251–55 indicates that the situation was probably more complicated than indicated in a two-stage development. For the purposes of this essay, however, identifying the two major contexts is sufficient.

33. Zahavy, *Studies in Jewish Prayer*, 87.

Stage 2: Between Jesus and Q²

So within years of Jesus' death, if not during his lifetime, some intrepid collector or collectors began gathering his oral legacy and committing it to writing. It is perhaps appropriate to apply the second-century word of Papias to this stage, "Matthew collected the sayings in the Hebrew language, and each interpreted them as best he could."[34] Jesus' sayings existed originally in Aramaic (Papias' "Hebrew"), but were partially in Greek as early as Q¹.

Numerous attempts at retrotranslation (from Greek to Aramaic or Hebrew) have been made over the last century. Notable are the efforts of Dalman, Jeremias, Fitzmyer, and de Moor.[35] Whereas Dalman, Jeremias, and Fitzmyer had attempted to recover the "everyday" speech of Jesus, de Moor places the Prayer within the sphere of "literary Aramaic." Here is something like the Aramaic exemplar for Q² (following Fitzmyer):

34. Eusebius, *Eccl. Hist.* 3.39.16. Kloppenborg is extremely skeptical, *Formation of Q*, 51–54.

35. Dalman, "Anhang A: Das Vaterunser," in *Die Worte Jesu*, 283–365; Jeremias, "The Lord's Prayer in Modern Research"; Fitzmyer, *Luke*, vol. 2, 901; de Moor, "Reconstruction," 403 n. 17. See Davies and Allison, "Excursus," 593. Meier (*A Marginal Jew*, 2:291–302) believes that there was an original Aramaic prayer stemming from Jesus. For an attempt to discover a Hebrew exemplar of the Prayer, see Young, *Jewish Background*.

Figure 3.2: The Lord's Prayer in Aramaic

	Address	*'abba'*
		Father
Table 1	Petition 1	*ythqdsh shmk*
		may your name be sanctified
	Petition 2	*thîthî mlkûthk*
		may your kingdom come
Table 2	Petition 4	*lḥmn'a dîmsthî'a*
		hb lnâ yôm'a dnâ
		the bread of sufficiency
		give us this day
	Petition 5	*ûshbôq lnâ ḥôbîn'a*
		kdî shbqn'a lḥîbîn'a
		and release our debts
	Petition 6	just as we release our debtors
		wl'a th'alînn'a lnsiyôn
		and please do not bring us to
		the test

Since various assumptions have to come into play, consensus about reconstruction has not been achieved. Variations in the modern retrotranslations appear especially in the second table. Fitzmyer aptly writes: "The reconstruction of the original Aramaic form of the 'Our Father' will always remain problematic, conditioned above all by our knowledge of the Palestinian Aramaic of Jesus' days."[36] Not only the Aramaic, but also the meaning of the Greek controlling the Aramaic retrotranslation is obscure. Though consensus may not be possible, certain details in the tradition are thrown into relief.

The evidence of Paul and Mark on the use of *'abba'* supplies important information regarding this period of the Prayer's history. Since the Lord's Prayer inculcates an election consciousness that bespeaks immediacy with God, these two writers seem generally familiar with Jesus' characteristic understanding of God (Luke 10:21–22 [Q]; Rom 8:15–16; Mark 1:10–11; 14:36). Mark 11:25 and 14:36 also

36. Fitzmyer, *Luke*, vol. 2, 901.

seem to echo the third and fifth petitions, but neither Paul nor Mark quotes the entire Prayer. How should its absence in their texts be understood?

As the Corinthian correspondence, Romans 15, and Acts make clear, Paul was widely traveled, and it would be difficult now to determine with precision where he came into contact with particular streams of early Jesus traditions. By a careful study of quotes and allusions, and keeping in mind Victor Paul Furnish's observation about Paul's rare use of Jesus in contrast to the Old Testament,[37] we can make the following observations:

1) Paul seems only fragmentarily to have known Q in its distinctive Galilean form (i.e., Wisdom Q). First Corinthians 9:14 and 10:27 allude to Luke 10:7, 8 respectively. These seem to be the only places where Paul connects with Q^1. Perhaps one of the factions of Corinth possessed a copy, in view of the general concern for wisdom there. However, Paul's failure to mention the Prayer where it might be beneficial (e.g., 1 Corinthians 11 in reference to the communal difficulties surrounding the meal of association, when such a Prayer might be offered) seems to speak against this, or at least Paul's knowledge of it.

2) Paul otherwise is more familiar with "Judean" elements of the synoptics, as when he refers in 1 Cor 7:10–11 to something like Mark 10:11 (Divorce and Remarriage) or in 1 Cor 11:23–25 to something like Luke 22:17–19 (Giving Thanks over Cup and Bread). Already in 1 Thess 5:2, 4 there is contact with Luke 12:39 [Q] (Like A Thief in the Night) or Mark 13:35–36 (The Master Arrives in the Night). Elsewhere (Rom 12:14, 17), Paul shows familiarity with traditions like Luke 6:27, 29 / Matt 5:39–44 [Q] and in a fashion that would suggest concern for Antiochene Torah interpretation. Concerns with marital purity, Jerusalem traditions of the Last Supper, Torah interpretation, and apocalyptic timetables we would expect from a former Pharisee (Gal 1:14; Phil 3:5) who received significant elements of

37. "[O]ne must concede the relative sparsity of direct references to or citations of Jesus' teachings in the Pauline letters. The argument that he could presuppose his readers' familiarity with these because he had already passed them on in his missionary preaching is not convincing. He could and does presuppose knowledge of the Old Testament, but this in no way deters him from constantly and specifically citing it in the course of his ethical teaching," Furnish, *Theology and Ethics in Paul*, 55.

his knowledge about Jesus from the Jerusalem church (1 Cor 11:23; 15:3).[38]

Mark, while still remaining unfamiliar with the majority of Q's contents, had more substantial contact with them (how is unclear). This can be seen, for instance, in Mark's knowledge of Q: Luke 3:2–4; 3:16–17; 4:1–2; 10:4–11 (cf. Paul); 11:14–23; 13:18–19. As in Q[2], Mark also evinces a prophet christology (e.g., Mark 1:1, 8, 10; Luke 6:23 [Q]; 7:31–35 [Q]), shows conflict with Pharisees (Mark 2:16; Q elements of Luke 11:39–52), a heightened concern with purity issues (Mark 7:1–2, 14–15; Luke 11:39–41 [Q]), and apocalyptic-eschatological preoccupations (e.g., "son of man" preoccupations as at Mark 14:62; Luke 12:8 [Q]). Paul was not familiar with the bulk of this material (absence of "son of man" material in Paul is particularly striking), so a time after Paul for Q[2] seems appropriate. Mark, however, clearly had contact with or at least shared interests with the later Q tradents.

Q[1], therefore, did not contain the Lord's Prayer, or contained the Lord's Prayer (Kloppenborg) which however remained unknown to Paul and Mark. These both were substantially linked to Jerusalem–Judean traditions. Paul remained largely ignorant of Galilean Jesus materials, though Mark had access to Galilean miracle stories and ideas similar to those of Q[2].[39] As the two-source hypothesis has long urged, extensive Jesus materials were mediated independently to Matthew, Luke, and John(?) through at least two separate lineages of Judean-oriented scribes (Mark, Q). Q was a Galilean source, but with Judean interests. Unless the "secret teaching" hypothesis is embraced, the Lord's Prayer would seem to have been largely unknown or only imperfectly known to Jerusalem-Judean sources (available to Paul and Mark) until the later first century.

Stage 1: The Setting of Jesus

The Lord's Prayer existed in a much simpler form in the context of Jesus and the earliest Jesus movement, and grew by certain measurable

---

38. Compare Betz's assessment of these issues, and additional bibliography, *Sermon on the Mount*, 6 and n. 12.

39. Theissen, *Gospels in Context*, 99.

developments into the forms we have come to know today.[40] The differences in form are best accounted for by differing scribal traditions and interests.

Some further decisions are necessary about the form of the Prayer for Jesus. The uniformity of the first table in contrast to the second at the Q^2 stage suggests that the former was extremely conventional and perhaps extant only in Greek, while the latter offered difficulties of interpretation indicative of the earlier move from Aramaic to Greek. Besides uniformity in the Greek, various other considerations argue against the first table having belonged originally to the Prayer of Jesus; chief among them are linguistic, internal theological, and external social considerations. Linguistically, the first table adopts the more polite jussive ("let," "may"), while the imperatives of the second table are coarse and direct. Theologically, there is great tension between Jesus' own *Abba*-consciousness and Petitions 1, 2, or 3; as well, the abstractions of the first table (God's name, kingdom, and will) militate against the concrete and mundane concerns in Jesus' Prayer. Sociologically, the first table stands in clear relationship to later synagogue prayer traditions and thus is an understandable accretion.

Taussig points out that 'abba' stands uneasily over against the first petition. He characterizes this tension as deriving from either Jesus or someone closer to Q: "The irony of an occasional juxtaposition of the familiar 'abba' with the next phrase 'May your name be holy' certainly could have been appreciated by a witty aphorizer."[41] A comparable tension, however, is evident between the second petition and the address. An immediate consciousness of God and concern for God's direct involvement in the moment (second table) are *both* difficult to reconcile with purity (Petition 1) and eschatology (Petition 2).

A generation ago, Jeremias pointed out the connection between the Lord's Prayer and the *Qaddish*. He can be criticized today for a rather anachronistic employment of this material, since there is

---

40. There are similarities between the approach of this essay and the views of Lohmeyer, who distinguished a Galilean from a Jerusalem form of the Prayer. We work with a more developed relation of the Prayer to social context.

41. Taussig, "The Lord's Prayer," 33.

debate as to the antiquity of the prayer.[42] Jeremias argued that the form of the *Qaddish* validated the shorter Lukan form of the prayer, even though all three of Matthew's first-table petitions are contained within the *Qaddish*:

> *Exalted and hallowed be his great name* in the world which he created *according to his will.*
>
> May he let his *kingdom rule (etc.)*
>
> [Our Father who are in heaven, let your name be *sanctified,* let your *kingdom come,* let your *will be done (etc.)*]

Clearly the *Qaddish* is related to the late-synoptic forms of the Lord's Prayer. There are also perceptible links between the Lord's Prayer and the *Amidah* (or *Shemoneh Esreh,* "Eighteen Benedictions").[43] As Zahavy's discussion of the social origins of these materials indicates, Jerusalem-Judean interests are in view, with the implication that the Lord's Prayer was augmented at the Q^2 stage for better alignment with Judean scribal interests.

While Taussig and The Jesus Seminar have tended to read Jesus too much in relation to Socrates, Jesus' concerns can with greater historical logic be seen to stand solidly within the orbit of Israelite tradition, have much more to do with Moses than Socrates, and define Jesus as a particular type of first-century "Jew." This is evident in a perceptible link between the Lukan beatitudes (the first sapiential compositional unit in Q^1) and the Aramaic beginning of the Passover Haggadah:[44]

---

42. Baumgardt, "Kaddish and Lord's Prayer," 165, dependent upon Elbogen, *Der jüdische Gottesdienst,* notes that the *Qaddish* is attested no earlier than the Byzantine period. De Moor, "Reconstruction," 405 n. 26 claims that the "antiquity of the prayer is recognized by all authorities" and appeals to *b. Ber.* 3a (R. Jose b. Halaphta, ca. 150 CE) and *Sipre* 306 (132b). Lachs, "The Lord's Prayer," 118, considers that the *Qaddish* is too dissimilar to the Lord's Prayer to provide a convincing parallel and that the tannaitic "short prayer" (*tpîllâ qṣrâ*) provides a more appropriate genre.

43. Lachs, "The Lord's Prayer," 118 and 123 n. 1; Davies and Allison, "Excursus," 595–97.

44. The Passover Haggadah is the narrative of the Exodus told during Passover meal (Seder). A fuller statement about this connection is made in Oakman, "Archaeology of First-Century Galilee," orig. 220–51.

PASSOVER HAGGADAH	BEATITUDES
The bread of poverty	How honorable are you poor[45]
Let all who are hungry	How honorable are the hungry
This year we are here	How honorable are those who mourn

Likewise, the second discourse in Luke 10:4 [Q[1]] contains a possible (albeit negative) allusion to Exod 12:11. Ezekiel the Tragedian, of the second century BCE, already showed a concern for this text in the Hellenistic period:

> your loins girt up and shoes upon your feet, and in your hand a staff, for thus in haste the king will order all to leave the land. It shall be called "Passover."[46]

It is clear in comparing Mark's to Q's "discourses" that the respective traditions have situated these instructions within a less focused mission for the kingdom of God. Mark's tradition would thus seem to be closer to Jesus given an original Passover or Passover pilgrimage setting for the material. The injunctions about money, bag, food, and clothing suggest dependence upon hospitality along the pilgrim's way, perhaps reflecting trust that God will provide for the pilgrim. Galilean "Jews" seem to have been particularly attracted to the Passover pilgrimage. Jesus alluded to Exodus imagery in stating the meaning of his own healing activity (Luke 11:20 [Q]; cf. Exod 8:19). And Jesus' Last Supper (even if not a Passover meal) is clearly tied to the great festival within the synoptic tradition.

While this is not the place to develop a full-blown account of the "theology of Jesus," a few remarks will make intelligible the exegetical approach taken below toward the Lord's Prayer. Jesus' preaching of the kingdom is universally conceded by scholars to be the center of his historical message.[47] The interests of Jesus in Passover and Exodus, as well as the early prophet christologies, would suggest that he meant by "kingdom of God" something like the "lord-

---

45. On translating the opening term as "honorable" rather than "blessed," see K. C. Hanson, "'How Honorable!' 'How Shameful.'"

46. *Ezek. Trag.* 181–184, according to Robertson, "Ezekiel the Tragedian," 816. Cf. Mark 6:8–9, which is closer to the injunction of Ezekiel.

47. Jeremias, *New Testament Theology*, 96. Perrin, *Rediscovering*, 47, points to the close linkage between kingdom of God and the Prayer.

ship of God" over historical affairs and looked for something like an Exodus from "Egypt," representing what must have been felt to be oppressive circumstances of his first-century environment. Jesus was not a scripture specialist, however, and seemed to flesh out his theology as a kind of village wisdom preacher more with reference to the natural order of things.[48] Both aspects (concern with Moses and natural theological wisdom) allow us to understand how the peasant Jesus could inspire Wisdom Q as well as Deuteronomic Q and apocalyptic Mark.

This picture seems corroborated by indications of Josephus about typical, lower-class theological concerns around the Lake of Galilee. During the early phases of the Judean–Roman War, Jesus son of Sapphias had led an attack by the lower classes of Tiberias against Herod Antipas's palace, in which were animal representations, and thus offending their sensibilities about "no graven images."[49] Half a century earlier, Judas of Gamala had urged that payment of Roman taxes was a sign of servitude to alien gods.[50] If Judas of Gamala brought to expression the rage of at least some Galilean peasantry, who could be convinced that Roman Palestine might be a new Egypt, then Jesus of Nazareth operating in the vicinity naturally might have shared similar religious interests and orientations. His interests and concerns stand at the root of a complex of traditions, not only Q[1], but also Q[2], Paul, Mark, and even John. Elaborations of these traditions have to be kept in the discussion about Jesus' theological and social outlooks. The Lord's Prayer, nonetheless, can certainly be understood as an expression of familiarity with the God of Exodus.[51] Its meaning thus can be investigated within a developmental frame that expanded Jesus' concrete requests in definite directions.

48. Oakman, *Jesus and the Economic Questions*, 240–42.

49. Josephus, *Life* 65–67; see Exod 20:4.

50. Josephus, *War* 2.118; *Ant.* 18. 4.

51. Cyster, "The Lord's Prayer and the Exodus Tradition," provides a rather popular treatment of this idea.

The Social Meaning of the Lord's Prayer

Three major stages of development of the Lord's Prayer have thus been suggested, now listed in chronological order:

Stage 1: The form of the prayer in Jesus' own usage, consisting of the address + Petitions 4–6;

Stage 2: the difficult-to-trace transition from oral-Aramaic to written-Greek forms of the Prayer; and

Stage 3: the form of the Prayer reached by the latest stratum of Q (as seen in Luke), consisting of the address + Petitions 1–2 + Petitions 4–6.

Matthew and *Didache*, indicative of late first-century Syrian tradition, subsequently carried things further by the addition of expanded address, Petitions 3 and 7, plus the doxology. These presumptions now come into play in pursuit of the social meaning of the Lord's Prayer, first for Jesus and then for the later tradents of the Jesus traditions.

The Address

Luke's version of the address stands closest to the actual speech of Jesus. The emphatic and simple address, in contrast to Matthew's version that reflects more nearly the formal conventions of synagogue prayer, is noteworthy.[52] Jeremias argued for the uniqueness within Judaism, as well as the intimacy, of addressing God as *'abba'*, "Papa," but both claims are disputed today.[53]

Whether intimate or simply direct, the Prayer addresses as *pater familias*, "head of the household," the One who is also expected to rule as King. The petitioner acts as a royal personage and heir, a part of the royal household.[54] The generosity and benevolence of the King are invoked, who acts as Patron. This assumption of the graciousness and benevolence of God comes through at several other points in the Jesus tradition. One thinks, for instance, of the Prodigal Son/Father

52. Jeremias, *Prayers*, 96–97.

53. Davies and Allison, "Excursus," 601–2; Barr, "Abba Isn't Daddy."

54. This will have further implications in the discussion of the bread petition.

(L/Luke 15:11–32). There are also passages like Matt 5:45 (M); Luke 11:11–13 (Q); 12:30 (Q); and Mark 10:30.[55] In Jesus' context, the concern for God's patronage in relation to concrete need was underscored by immediate transition to the petitions of the second table.

Petition 4 of the Second Table

The general concern of Jesus and the early Jesus movement for the hungry is manifest directly in the feeding narratives (e.g., Mark 6:34–44) and indirectly by a number of other gospel passages. For instance, many of the people "healed" by Jesus were perhaps suffering the effects of malnutrition. These were typically people with skin ailments or eye problems (Mark 1:40–45; 10:46; cf. 5:43 and Matt 6:22–23 [Q])—perhaps due simply to vitamin deficiencies. One must emphasize, therefore, the therapeutic significance, in a physical as well as a social sense, of table fellowship for the Jesus movement (Mark 2:15). This fellowship was probably the primary setting in life of the first petition of Jesus' Prayer, a table fellowship I have elsewhere argued was tied to Passover concerns.[56]

Interpreting the petition for bread has long been vexed by the question surrounding the meaning of the word *epiousios* (ordinarily translated as "daily"). Questions were already raised in the days of Origen (185–254), who believed the word was a neologism of the evangelists. On the basis of current philology, Origen's judgment appears to be correct.[57]

Four major solutions to the issue of meaning have been suggested over the centuries: 1) That of Origen, Chrysostom, and others tracing the etymology of *epiousios* to *epi* + *ousia* = "necessary for

55. Kloppenborg, "Literary Convention," 89. See Malina, *The Social World of Jesus and the Gospels*, 143–75.

56. Oakman, "Archaeology of First-Century Galilee," 243–44.

57. BAGD, 297; BDF 66 §123. See, however, the cautionary remarks of Deissmann, *Light From the Ancient East*, 78, whose experience with the papyri led him to suspect any "neologistic" approaches to biblical Greek. He offered a slightly different opinion in his *Bible Studies*, 214. Hemer, "*Epiousios*," attempts to find a good Greek lineage for *epiousios*. He follows Lightfoot and argues strenuously for Solution 3, "the following day." For a thorough discussion of previous philological solutions, see Foerster, "Ἐπιούσιος."

existence"; 2) that of Debrunner seeing an analogy with the phrase *epi tēn ousan* [sc. *hēmeran*], "for the current day"; 3) that of Grotius, Wettstein, and Lightfoot connecting the adjective with the Greek phrase *hē epiousa* [sc. *hēmera*], "the following day"; 4) finally, that of Cyril of Alexander, Peter of Laodicea, and others linking *epiousios* with the verb *epienai* "coming in the future."[58] There are subvarieties of these major solutions; all but 1) assume a temporal meaning of some sort.

The two somewhat different solutions proposed here build upon Origen's suggestion and basic interpretation. However, the meaning is not sought in the philosophical use of *ousia*, i.e., "being, existence, substance," but in the usages attested in many of the Egyptian papyri. The word *ousia* in the papyri often means "landed estate" or "large estate."[59] This is a concrete meaning rooted in the material realities of antiquity. If *epiousios* is a neologism reflecting a Semitic idiom, it makes sense to look for something in Aramaic incorporating the notion of "estate." The papyri, as purveyors of a more popular idiom, are more likely than Greek philosophy to give a clue to the meaning of *epiousios*.

Warrant for this philological procedure is given by considering the New Testament unique term, *periousios*, a word linguistically near in kinship to *epiousios*.[60] While *periousios* clearly means "chosen" in

---

58. BAGD, 297.

59. Moulton and Milligan, 242, s.v. επιουσιος, and 467, s.v. ουσια. Moulton once wrote (Moulton and Howard, *Grammar*, 2:313): "the only meaning quotable for this noun [sc. ουσια] from NT and papyri is property or estate, which is not hopeful." Moulton could see no way to elucidate the meaning of *epiousios* from the papyri. He did, however, recognize (91) that the lack of elision between *epi* and *ousia* would constitute no barrier to Solution 1: "The Hellenistic indifference to the confluence of vowels, due to the slower pronunciation which has been already noted, is well seen . . . This feature of the *Koine* makes it very plain that classical scholars of the last generation were yielding to their besetting sin when they ruled out (e.g.) etymologies of *epiousios* that broke the laws of 'correctness' by allowing hiatus." Recently, Fitzmyer, *Luke*, vol. 2, 900, has endorsed the use of Solution 1 with these words: "After long consideration, I have reverted to the explanation given by Origen . . ."

60. Titus 2:14, quoting Deut 14:2 (LXX). Origen already noted this parallel, observing the underlying material implications of both words in ordinary speech but arguing for the "spiritual" meaning of *epiousios* in view of the use of *periousios* in Titus.

Titus 2:14, its meaning in the Septuagint is tied more literally to the Hebrew word *sglâ* = "possession, property," and in very late Hebrew "treasure."[61] Thus, in Eccl 2:8 (LXX) "Solomon" talks about having gathered "gold and silver, and treasures (*periousiasmous*) of kings and countries." In the Greek papyri, *periousios* means "abundance, superfluity." An excellent example of the use of this word from approximately the same time as the Prayer of Jesus was being translated from Aramaic into Greek is given by the famous rescript of Claudius to the Judean community in Alexandria, Egypt (ca. 41 CE):

> I explicitly order the Judeans not to agitate for more privileges than they formerly possessed . . . while enjoying their own privileges and sharing a great abundance [*periousias*] of advantages in a city not their own . . .[62]

Periousias in some cases in the Septuagint and in the secular usage of the papyri occurs in contexts reflecting material abundance. A similar sphere of meaning can be suggested for *epiousios*.[63]

Thus, the first proposal offered here is that *epiousios* is simply a synonym for *periousios* as used in the papyri, which would lead to the meaning for the fourth petition, "give us today bread in abundance." The implication is that adequate bread is not available, and the Divine Patron is approached for immediate redress. Since several of the ancient Israelite apocalypses expected the end time to be a time of great abundance, it is not difficult to see how this petition might later (in Q) have connected with eschatological themes.[64]

A related inquiry (proposal two) might pursue some Semitic idiom behind the word *epiousios*. Fitzmyer, presuming Origen's basic view, cites Prov 30:8 "the food I need" (*lḥm ḥqî*). In the Aramaic targum this is expressed *lḥm'a <d> msthî*. Fitzmyer consequently offers as a translation for his reconstruction of the Aramaic form of the

61. BDB, 688; Jastrow, *Dictionary*, 953.

62. Hunt and Edgar, *Select Papyri*, 2:87; Moulton and Milligan, *Vocabulary*, 507.

63. *Epi* often means "in addition, above" (in a figurative sense), BAGD, 287. *Peri* in *periousios* is synonymous with *hyper*: Moulton and Howard, *Grammar*, 321. The adverb *enousiōs* also provides an analogy, meaning "very rich"; LSJ, 572, 1439.

64. E.g., *1 Enoch* 10; *2 Bar.* 29:5.

bread petition: "Give us this day our bread for subsistence."[65] This concrete meaning (as opposed to Origen's abstraction of "supersubstantial" bread) undoubtedly appealed to peasants. Again, "peasant" included not only agriculturalists, but also their impoverished relatives eking out a living in lowly building trades or the fishing syndicates by the lake.[66]

Perhaps there is yet another option related to this line of inquiry: A correspondence might be established between *epi* and the Aramaic particle *dî*. Both the Greek preposition and the Aramaic particle can serve to mark the genitive case in their respective languages.[67] Hence, there may be nothing more than a simple possessive sense demanded by the *epi*: "Belonging to the estate or property." In Dan 2:15, for instance, the Aramaic reads "the king's captain" (*shlit'a di-mlk'a*). In the Septuagint, this is translated by a simple genitive case. However, in the case of *epiousios* a very literal correspondence between the languages has evidently been maintained. It might also be an attempt to avoid ambiguities which would result from making a genitival adjective out of *ousia*, the stem of which ends in *iota*.

Such a wooden Greek translation may have signposted a meaning integral to Jesus' understanding of *'abba'*: The patron made regular provision for those already on the estate ("the kingdom"). A suggestive late-Hebrew parallel is at hand in *Ruth Rab.* 2:14. There reference is made to "bread belonging to the kingdom," or "the royal maintenance" (*lhm shl mlkût*).[68] *Ousia* in the Egyptian papyri can signify an imperial estate. *Epiousios* with this connotation would then give the following sense for the fourth petition: "Give us the bread of the kingdom today," or perhaps "Give us the royal bread ra-

65. Fitzmyer, *Luke*, vol. 2, 900–901.

66. Oakman, "Was Jesus a Peasant?" 117–18; K. C. Hanson, "The Galilean Fishing Economy and the Jesus Tradition."

67. "A genuine Aram. idiom," according to BDB, 1088. The corresponding particle in late Hebrew is *sh*, which shows the influence of Aramaic: "in usage limited to late Heb., and passages with N. Palest. colouring," BDB, 979. Cf. Jastrow, *Dictionary*, 1577. A literal equivalence would pair *epi* with Aramaic ʿ*al* = "upon." Turner, *A Grammar of New Testament Greek*, 271 shows that during the New Testament period *epi* was fast becoming a marker of the accusative case rather than the genitive case. The ratios for various bodies of literature (taken from Turner) are: (Papyri) 4.5 [gen.]::2.5 [acc.], (NT) 1.2::2, (LXX) 1.4::3.8.

68. Jastrow, *Dictionary*, 704.

tion today." An even more colloquial rendition, taken in conjunction with the suggested interpretation of the address, might be: "Give us today bread on the house." These are words spoken by the King's own children, addressed to their benevolent Father.

(Secondary: Petition 1 of the First Table)

Abundant or "estate-bread" was of immediate concern to Jesus and his disciples, but the Q tradition moved toward greater theological abstraction. If the Lord's Prayer belonged to Wisdom Q, then the concrete concerns above were still evident in Luke 11:9–13 [Q] (better preserved at the end in Matt 7:11). A later concern about idolatry in Deuteronomic Q (Luke 4:3–4, 7–8 [Q]) pushed the meaning of the Prayer toward a concern for purity of the name (Luke 11:2 [Q]) and eventually enacting God's righteous will on earth (Matt 6:10). Q and Mark would then align Jesus' interests more clearly with the prophetic traditions of Israel, and this also involved the purity and eschatological concerns evident in later first-century Israelite prayers.

A general distance, though clear connection, between Jesus and the interests of Judean-Jerusalem scribes can be traced. Careful study of *hagiazein* ("sanctify," "make holy"), which appears in the New Testament in 1 Thessalonians, 1 Corinthians, Romans, Matthew, Luke, John, Acts, Ephesians, 1–2 Timothy, Hebrews, 1 Peter, and Revelation, shows that the word signifies New Testament materials with clear links to temple or Judean-Jerusalem interests (Paul, later gospels and Acts, Deutero-Paulines, Hebrews, and Revelation). The lack of such links in early Q (Q¹), and the unlikelihood of such interests for peasant Galileans, is therefore worth note.[69]

The accretion of Petition 1 by the time of later Q (Q²) moves the Prayer more tightly into the orbit of Judean interests. What is meant by sanctification of the name in early Judaism? Jeremias connects this petition (and the second) with the previously mentioned Jewish *Qaddish* prayer and believes that both prayers make entreaty for

---

69. Meier, *A Marginal Jew*, vol. 2, 295–98, notes that "The idea of hallowing (sanctifying, making holy) the name of God is totally absent from the rest of the Synoptic sayings of Jesus . . ."

> the revelation of God's eschatological kingdom . . . They
> seek the hour in which God's profaned and misused
> name will be glorified and his reign revealed, in accor-
> dance with the promise, "I will vindicate the holiness of
> my great name, which has been profaned among the na-
> tions . . ." (Ezek 36:23)[70]

Jeremias' understanding, however, does not go far enough. For
Jeremias and for many twentieth-century commentators, the first
petition is only a prayer bidding God to sanctify his own name in an
eschatological sense.

Yet even the *Qaddish* suggests a more extended significance:
"Exalted and hallowed be his great name *in the world* . . ." *Who* it
is who will "sanctify the name," and *where* this will happen, are the
critical questions. The *Qaddish* implies that human, in addition to
divine action, and actions in the world, are critical for the issue of
sanctification.

This impression is borne out by a study of the idiom "sanctify the name" in rabbinic traditions.[71] The Piel form of the Hebrew
verb *qdsh*, just as the Pael in Aramaic, can specify human activity
as sanctification of the name. *B. Soṭa* refers to Joseph's sanctifying
deed; *Sipra* 18, 6 (339a) refers to Israel's obligation; and the third
benediction of the *Amidah* enjoins such human activity without
specifying precise content. Later midrash is rich in illustration. In
Genesis Rabbah Abraham says, "I will go forth and fall [in battle] in
sanctifying the name of the Holy One, Blessed be He."[72] The Levites
were believed to have given their lives slaughtering the unfaithful to
sanctify the name.[73] The suffering of the exile is an occasion for sanctifying the name.[74] God's name can also be sanctified when justice is

---

70. Jeremias, *Prayers*, 99.

71. In addition to what is laid out here, see the material gathered in Str-B.
1:411–18 ("Menschen als Subjekt des Heiligens").

72. *Gen. Rab.* 43:2 (1: 352) [Numbers in parentheses refer to the volume
and page in Freedman and Simon, *Midrash Rabbah*]. Abraham in the fiery
furnace, *Gen. Rab.* 63:2 (2: 557); *Lev. Rab.* 11:7 (4: 144); *Num. Rab.* 2:12 (5:43);
Eccl. Rab. 2:14:1 (8: 64). Jastrow, *Dictionary*, s.v. *qdsh*.

73. *Num. Rab.* 1:12 (5:19–20); 4:6 (5:100).

74. *Num. Rab.* 13:2 (6:501); cf. *Gen. Rab.* 98: 14 (2:964).

accomplished in human affairs.[75] Most of these instances illustrate *in extremis* that fidelity unto death or punishment by death can sanctify the name. This observation is documented perhaps most completely by a midrashic passage about the martyrs at the time of the Bar Kochba revolt (132–35 CE):

> The Rabbis say: He [*sc.* God] adjured them by the generation of the great persecution. They are called *zebaoth* because they carried out My will (*zibyoni*) in the world and through them My will was executed; and HINDS OF THE FIELD because they poured out their blood for the sanctification of My Name . . . R. Ḥiyya b. Abba said: If one should say to me, "Sacrifice your life for the sanctification of God's name," I am ready to do so, on condition only that they slay me at once, but I could not endure the tortures of the great persecution.[76]

Other lesser human actions can sanctify the name of God. Blessing is one such action. In the Babylonian Talmud we read, "A benediction which contains no mention of the Divine Name is no benediction."[77] The Passover Meal begins with a blessing of the name: "Blessed art thou, O Lord our God, creator of the fruit of the vine."[78] This connection between human blessing and divine sanctification is further cemented by the *Qaddish* at the beginning of the Sabbath service in the Jewish Prayer Book:

> Glorified and *sanctified* be God's great name throughout the world which he has created according to his will. May he establish his kingdom in your lifetime and during your days, and within the life of the entire house of Israel, speedily and soon; and say, Amen.

75. David wipes out Saul's family: *Num. Rab.* 8:4 (5: 219). Punishment of the unfaithful of Jerusalem by Nebuchadnezzar: *Lam. Rab.* 2:1:3 (7:155).

76. *Cant. Rab.* 2:7:1 (9: 113). Incidentally, the parallel between God's will and sanctification of the name is again established. On the date of the great persecution, see *Cant. Rab.* 2.5.3 (9:106 n. 2). However, compare *Cant. Rab.* 2.7.1 (9: 115) where "great persecution" refers to days before "Ben Koziba."

77. *B. Ber.* 40b, quoted. in Smith, "Lord's Prayer," 155.

78. A reading from Genesis is placed just before this blessing when Passover coincides with the Sabbath. See Glatzer, ed., *The Passover Haggadah*, 17.

> May his great name *be blessed* forever and to all eternity.
> Blessed and praised, glorified and exalted, extolled and
> honored, adored and lauded be the name of the Holy
> One, blessed be he, beyond all the blessings and hymns,
> praises and consolations that are ever spoken in the
> world; and say, Amen.[79]

Many other such blessings—and the firm connection between blessing and God's name—can be seen throughout the devotional literature of the Jewish people. Furthermore, the Mishnah gives a rather
detailed picture of the events and situations that elicit blessings.[80]
Many of these blessings are connected with food and the meeting of
material need.

The first petition of the first table is secondary, therefore, though
in some senses it forms a logical development out of the bread petition. If the fourth petition prayed for the concrete situation that
would evoke such blessings of the name, then blessing God for the
reception of food can be one of the concrete meanings of "sanctifying
the Name." This may indeed be one understanding of the tradition
in the synoptics (heavily influenced by Judean-Jerusalem scribal
interests), as evident in Jesus' words around bread-breaking (Matt
14:19; 26:26; and par.) and *Didache's* association of the Prayer with
the Lord's Supper. Q[2] played a significant role in these developed
meanings of the Lord's Prayer, for while it does not directly mention
a concern with the *Shema* (as Mark 12:29–30), it does show concern
with Israel's integrity and fidelity to God (Luke 3:8; 4:4 [Q]):

79. Birnbaum, ed., *Daily Prayer Book*, 50 (italics mine). The Jewish Prayer
Book or Siddur, provides set prayers for various occasions throughout the year
and, although modern, contains much very old and traditional material such
as the Qaddish.

80. *M. Ber.* 6–9.

P. 1	May your name be sanctified	Q²	[*sc.* world ordered in accord with the *Shema*ᶜ]

Matthew [*sc.* in the act of blessing, in piety]

Post-70 Synagogue

Jesus

P. 4   Give us bread in abundance today *or*

Give us the bread of the kingdom today   [patronage resulting from exclusive allegiance and the ground for blessing]

Petition 5 of the Second Table

The fifth petition of Jesus' Prayer gives a critical clue as to what brought about this situation of want and hunger (not to mention we surmise the cursing of God's name because of physical deprivation). An agrarian context in which indebtedness prevails is a social context that will be characterized by an increasing level of impoverishment and hunger. Lack of bread coupled with debt presented a familiar constellation for Jesus and his peasant contemporaries.

Agrarian debt was pushing the peasantry of Jesus' day either entirely off the land (wage-labor on estates) or into client-dependency relations on the land vis-à-vis the Roman overlord (e.g., Caesar's large estates in the Esdraelon Plain or the land controlled by Judean-Herodian aristocrats in Sepphoris and Tiberias). The insecurity of the tenant or wage-laborer was evidenced in the increase in beggary and brigandage.[81] Brigands perhaps would have been more impressed by a zealot-like religious movement, but the activity of Jesus, which

81. See Horsley and J. S. Hanson, *Bandits, Prophets, and Messiahs*, 52–85; K. C. Hanson, "Jesus and the Social Bandits."

clearly shows concern for the beggar and disadvantaged, sought alternate ways to resolve class tensions and reconcile class interests.[82]

The Jesus tradition reveals an intimate acquaintance and concern with debt in the first half of the first century CE.[83] Q material alluding to debtor's prison (Luke 12:58–59/Matt 5:25–26), the story of the Unforgiving Slave (Matt 18:23–35 [M]), the parable of the Two Debtors (Luke 7:41–42 [L]), and the Widow's Coin (*lepta*, Mark 12:41–44) suggest this. The Parable of the Talents (Luke 19:12–27/Matt 25:14–30 [Q?]) and the Parable of the Steward of Unrighteousness (Luke 16:1–8 [L]) relate the oppressiveness of the creditor.

Outside of the New Testament, historical data for a debt problem in early Roman Palestine are supplied by the so-called *prozbul* of Hillel and an important passage in Josephus. One of the first acts of the insurgents in 66 CE was the burning of the record office where debt contracts were kept:

> [The rebels] next carried their combustibles to the public archives, eager to destroy the money-lenders' bonds and to prevent the recovery of debts, in order to win over a host of grateful debtors and to cause a rising of the poor against the rich . . .[84]

In the same context, Josephus refers to such archives as the "sinews" of the city, a telling metaphor.

The precise significance of the *prozbul* is not easily established. The *Mishnah* indicates that Hillel's measure was supposed to make credit easier to obtain. Loans were not being given on account of the seventh-year release, so Hillel ostensibly permitted a practice that would alleviate the cash flow crisis. According to *m. Sheb.* 10:2 and *b. Giṭ.* 37b, loan contracts "delivered to the court" are not canceled according to the seventh-year prescriptions of Deuteronomy 15. The "logic" behind this is that the letter of the law in Deut 15:3 demands "your hand shall release," but if the bonds are with the court, the letter does not apply. The development of this legal maneuver apparently

---

82. Oakman, *Jesus and the Economic Questions*, 210, 215.

83. See also Oakman "Jesus and Agrarian Palestine: The Factor of Debt" (chapter 2 above); *Jesus and the Economic Questions*, 72–77; and Goodman, "The First Jewish Revolt."

84. Josephus, *War* 2.427 (Thackeray, LCL).

resulted in the interpretation "before the court" commonly placed upon *prozbul* in later rabbinic tradition.[85]

Work of Ludwig Blau years ago offered a different insight into the meaning of *prozbul*. The Hebrew in the *Mishnah* in fact is *prôz-bôl*, sometimes *prôsbôl*.[86] Blau traced the etymology of the word back to the Greek *prosbolē*, which according to Egyptian papyri was the "knocking down" of mortgaged property. Blau's view has recently been revived by Hans von Kippenberg.[87] Furthermore, form-critical study of the Hillel legislation by Neusner has led him to believe that Hillel's name and scriptural warrants were only later attached to a legal institution firmly established prior to the second century CE. Debt documents from the Judean desert, for instance, show no knowledge of a stipulation along the lines of the later rabbinic view of the *prozbul*, but they do reveal that loans were secured by various kinds of property:

Murabba'at Contract 18 (ca. 55 CE):

> [On . . . of the month . . . in] the second year of Caesar Nero in Siwaya, Absalom, son of Hanin, from Siwaya agreed that he borrowed from him in his presence: I, Zechariah, son of Johanan, son of . . . resident in Chessalon, have received the money [as a loan] of 20 denarii. I will repay it on . . . and if I do not restitute it by this term, then it will be paid to you with a fifth, and it will be completely repaid on this sabbatical year ([alternately] though a sabbath year intervene). And if I should not do it, there will be a substitute for you out of my goods, and to that which I shall acquire, you have right of appropriation.[88]

Murabba'at Contract 22 (132 CE):

> On the fourteenth of Marheschwan, Year One of the liberation of Israel . . . [the sum] of 50 [denarii] in coins

85. Again *b. Git.* 37b. Cf. Blau, "Der Prosbol," 111.

86. Jastrow, *Dictionary*, 1218.

87. Von Kippenberg, *Religion und Klassenbildung*, 139. Cf. Preisigke, *Fachwörter*, 149; also LSJ, 1504.

88. Benoît et al., *Les Grottes de Murabba'at*, 1:100ff; Koffmahn, *Die Doppelurkunden*, 80–1. Cf. Neusner, *From Politics to Piety*, 17 n. 2.

according to the assessed valuation. This piece of ground of Chizqia is security for the payment [of the debt] to the value of . . .[89]

It can be concluded that the *prozbul* originally was a legal device whereby debts were secured by means of immovable property and foreclosure accomplished through a court proceeding. This practice went against the letter of the Mosaic law, which viewed the patrimonial lands of the clan as a permanent trust (Lev 25:23). Any land that had to be sold had to be redeemed under the old Israelite law (Lev 25:25–28). If the *prozbul* measure was "good" for urban artisans like the Pharisees and later rabbis, it could not have been as sympathetically perceived by rural folk. As Neusner observes: "Debtors . . . were here given a good motive to dislike Pharisees, who now rendered their debts into a perpetual burden."[90]

The fact that a Greek legal institution is here in view suggests three possible "entry points" into the legal practice of early Judaism: Ptolemaic Palestine, the later Hasmoneans (perhaps Jannaeus), or Herod. This legal institution, in any view, was a part of the social fabric of Jesus' period. Passages like 1 Macc 14:8 and 14:12 seem to indicate that the Maccabees were "pro-peasant." The picture in *Letter of Aristeas* (esp. 107ff), if it is to be dated around 100 BCE, confirms the agrarian prosperity of the early Hasmonean years. If under the first Hasmoneans the ancient Judean peasantry was in relatively good shape, by the second century CE its condition had deteriorated dramatically. There is evidence throughout the *Mishnah* of a large pool of "free" labor. Martin Goodman's book on Roman Galilee provides a start at analyzing the second-century social situation behind the tannaitic material.[91]

Stresses on rural lower-classes (including artisans and fishingfolk) were on the increase in turn-of-the-eras Palestine. In place of traditional peasants holding patrimonial land, tenants and wage-laborers were appearing, on the one hand, and large landed

---

89. Benoît et al., *Les Grottes de Murabbaʿat*, 1:118ff; Koffmahn, *Die Doppelurkunde*, 158–59. Kloppenborg indicates that the "execution clause" here was a standard feature of Greco-Roman legal contracts (private communication).

90. Neusner, *From Politics to Piety*, 16.

91. Goodman, *State and Society*.

proprietors, on the other. For these social realities the parables of Jesus give ample evidence. One of the chief mechanisms fueling this process of agrarian destruction was the burden of debt. Roman taxation (including the building programs of the Herods) and population increase contributed to this problem.

In a milieu in which debt of one sort or another was compromising the viability of life for many, the fifth petition of Jesus' prayer takes on a special vibrancy and urgency. The meaning of the petition assumes a "horizontal" and a "vertical" aspect. The horizontal meaning is concretely perceptible in both the Matthean and the Lukan versions of the second half of the petition:

Matthew: as we have released (or forgiven) our debtors.

Luke: for we ourselves are releasing (or forgiving) everyone in debt to us.

The meaning "release" for *aphiēmi* (Matthew perfect tense; Luke present tense) in a literal or concrete sense is clearly attested by Deut 15:3 (LXX).

How is the vertical aspect to be understood? It must be noted that Matthew has "Forgive us our *debts*," while Luke has "Forgive us our *sins*." The literal or concrete material understanding of the petition is not thwarted, because in Aramaic the same word means sin or debt (*ḥôbâ*). Also, the dative plural "for us" (*hēmin*) can best be understood as the dative of advantage (indicative of the general thrust of the original Aramaic).

There were perhaps two concrete situations in which God might be petitioned to achieve debt forgiveness for the advantage of the petitioner: 1) A court-system, perhaps one in which the *prozbul* held sway, and 2) the temple debt-system. Luke 12:58–59 [Q] likely refers to the courts within the jurisdiction of Herod Antipas. The passage makes clear that the debtor goes to court at a great disadvantage (ironically, petitioning the creditor as patron provides better "justice") and indicates that prisons stood ready to effect execution (cf. Matt 18:30, 34 [M]). Josephus and Philo show clearly how this mechanism worked: Debt prison forced the debtor's family to pay up![92]

---

92. Consider for instance the behavior of Albinus, Josephus, *War* 2.273.

The temple also imposed indebtedness upon Israelites. The temple tax was levied on all Israelite males over twenty years of age. The *Mishnah* indicates that ability to pay was not considered:

> On the 15th thereof the tables [of the money-changers] were set up in the provinces; and on the 25th thereof they were set up in the Temple. After they were set up in the Temple they began to exact pledges.[93]

Matthew 17:24–27 (M) certainly depicts a post-70 CE situation (v. 27a), but the pronouncement of v. 26 likely goes back to Jesus himself and fits well with the notion of debt forgiveness. In such a case, then, the fifth petition could request of the "owner of the house" (i.e., the temple) for release from the onerous obligations requisitioned each year by Judean authorities.

Another significant index of a concern about debt appears in the attention Jesus gives to disadvantaged groups—children (Mark 9:36), women forced into degrading social situations for economic reasons ("impure" Mark 5:25; prostitutes, Matt 21:31; widows, Mark 12:41–44), and others economically marginalized.[94] The case of the widow in Mark 12:41–44/Luke 21:1–4 is especially illuminating for the connection between economic marginalization and indebtedness. Why was the widow putting her money in the box at the temple? And was Jesus praising her generosity or lamenting her misfortune?[95]

There is compelling evidence that the widow's deposit in the temple was reason for lament. As Wright has convincingly observed, to think that Jesus praises the widow for depositing her "whole life" in the temple coffers directly contradicts Jesus' censure of the Pharisees over qorban vows (Mark 7:11–12). The principle enunciated there by Jesus brings out the priority of human need over temple piety. The same logic can be expected to apply in the case of the widow's coin.

Philo, *Spec. Laws* 3.30 recounts the extractions of an early first-century tax collector who laid hands on family members to force payment; see Lewis, *Life in Egypt under Roman Rule*, 161–62.

93. *M. Sheq.* 1:3 (Danby).

94. For a discussion of the connection between these groups and economic marginalization, see Schottroff and Stegemann, *Jesus and the Hope of the Poor*, 6–17; Stegemann and Stegemann, *The Jesus Movement*, 79–95.

95. Wright, "The Widow's Mites."

Whatever she may be doing for God by her temple sacrifice, she is thereby depriving herself and her orphaned children. Furthermore, Wright points out the significant connection in the synoptic tradition between this story and Jesus' saying immediately preceding it: "Beware of the Scribes . . . who devour widows' houses and for a pretext make long prayers" (Mark 12:38, 40).

Wright might have gone farther with this connection between "devouring widows' houses" and the widow's coin. There may in fact be grounds for restoring to some extent an aspect of praise in Jesus' word, although lament will also remain apparent, for there is another legislative tradition attached to the name of Hillel that perhaps brings a direct light upon the widow's action in Mark 12:41–44:

> If a man sold a house from among the houses in a walled city, he may redeem it at once and at any time during twelve months . . . Beforetime the buyer used to hide himself on the last day of the twelve months so that [the house] might be his for ever; but Hillel the Elder ordained that he [that sold it] could deposit his money in the [Temple] Chamber, and break down the door and enter, and that the other, when he would, might come and take his money.[96]

This tradition seems to pit Hillel against the scribes "who devour widows' houses," but it supplies a possible context for the widow's behavior and rationale for Jesus' observation as a mixture of lament and praise. The widow was demonstrating fidelity to her obligations to keep the house (which perhaps included land) in the family. Her deposit was, in this view, redemption money of some sort.

(Secondary: Petition 2 of the First Table)

In framing possible understandings of God's kingdom and will in the first table, emphases at the penultimate stage of the synoptic tradition indicate how Q and Markan prophetic understandings would flesh

96. Mishnah ʿArak. 9:3–4. This tradition is discussed in detail by Neusner, *From Politics to Piety*, 18–19. On temples as depositories for money preserving redemption rights, see Ginzberg, *Studies in the Economics of the Bible*, 62–63; see K. C. Hanson and Oakman, *Palestine in the Time of Jesus*.

out the Prayer of Jesus. Q² held a general concern for Israel's prophets, and linked John the Baptist and Jesus with their fate. John had been active at one point in Batanea, within the tetrarchy of Philip.⁹⁷ John was also associated with Perea and Herod Antipas's territory. Elijah had originated from Gilead (1 Kgs 17:1), and an Elijah–John the Baptist association came to be made at least in Mark (Mark 1:6). Since the Elijah-Elisha traditions had also showed concern for miraculous feedings (1 Kgs 17:6,16) and demonstrated special concern for widows (1 Kgs 17:8; 2 Kgs 4:1–7), these aspects of Jesus' activity were also highlighted by Mark (Mark 6:15; 8:28; 9:4, 11–13) and later Luke (4:26).

The precarious legal position of the widow in the ancient Near East was long recognized, especially in the wisdom tradition and the promulgations of kings.⁹⁸ Unlike the Greeks, many peoples of the ancient Near East believed that God or the gods and the powerful on earth had a special obligation toward widows and orphans. Thus, in the Old Testament:

> You shall not abuse any widow or orphan. If you do abuse them, when they cry out to me, I will surely hear their cry; my wrath will burn, and I will kill you with the sword, and your wives shall become widows and your children orphans. (Exod 22:22)

The Ugaritic story of Aqhat praises the wise man Daniel:

> Straightway Daniel the Rapha-man, Forthwith Ghazir [the Harna]miyy—[man], *Is upright*, [sitting before the g]at[e, Un]der [a mighty tree on the threshing floor, Judging] the cause [of the widow, Adjudicating] the case [of the fatherless.]⁹⁹

King Hammurabi (eighteenth century BCE) of Babylon boasts that he has protected the rights of widows and orphans.¹⁰⁰ In

97. Riesner, "Bethany beyond the Jordan," 704.

98. Especially helpful in understanding the widow's plight is the article by Stählin, "Χηρα."

99. Pritchard, ed., *The Ancient Near Eastern Texts*, 126.

100. Stählin, "Χηρα," 443 n. 31 for other ancient Near Eastern references.

Egyptian wisdom tradition, the "Instruction for King Meri-Ka-Re" (c. 2025–1700 BCE) admonishes:

> Do justice while you endure upon earth. Quiet the weeper; do not oppress the widow; supplant no man in the property of his father; and impair no officials at their posts.[101]

The connection of widow, property, and officials is significant since the "ancient oppression of widows at law may be seen in their frequent sale as slaves for debt," and "the main plight of widows was in the legal sphere."[102]

Later traditions continue to validate this picture quite precisely. The Qumran material from the Judean desert shows acute awareness of this problem:

> Unless they are careful to act in accordance with the exact interpretation of the law for the age of wickedness: to separate themselves from the sons of the pit; to abstain from wicked wealth which defiles, either by promise or by vow, and from the wealth of the temple and from stealing from the poor of the people, from making their widows their spoils and from murdering orphans . . .[103]

Goods of orphans might be valued by a Israelite court to meet their father's debt.[104] The property of widows was similarly vulnerable. A widow's marriage contract could be compromised if her husband dedicated his property to the temple. However, the rabbis stipulated that when the property was redeemed, the proceeds must go to meet the former contractual obligations of the husband to the wife. Debts and obligations, whether inherited from her former husband or forced upon her by circumstance, could seriously undermine the economic security of the widow in antiquity.

101. Pritchard, *Ancient Near Eastern Texts*, 415 (adapted).

102. Stählin, "Χηρα," 443, 445 respectively.

103. CD VI 14–17, according to García Martínez, *The Dead Sea Scrolls Translated*, 37.

104. M. ʿArak. 6:1.

Numbers Rabbah 21:12 relates that the inheritance of a woman changes hands only through judges.[105] The control of property in antiquity was a man's game. *Numbers Rabbah* 10:1 tells how a widow is forced to bring suit against her own son, although the precise issue at law is not clear.[106] Undoubtedly, the dispute is over property or the widow's maintenance—which are also concerns of early rabbinic discussions.[107] *Exodus Rabbah* 31:5 shows clearly that widows are oppressed by the lending at interest.[108]

The second petition now links Jesus' immediate and concrete concern for the oppressive affliction of little people with the sphere of royalty and the long-standing ancient Near Eastern traditions to place the weak under royal justice. As has been suggested on the basis of the *Qaddish*, the second petition for the coming of the kingdom of God emphasizes the (eschatological) hope for the manifestation of God's rule in the world. ʾAbbaʾ and the direct, second-person imperatives of the second table of the Prayer indicate God's immediacy to the needs of the petitioners. Wisdom Q also shared a much stronger sense of God's presence in Jesus' context. This immediacy is compromised a bit by a stronger eschatological sense of kingdom, which develops in the decades prior to the Judean–Roman War and is evident in Q[2] and Mark. Whereas Jesus and followers had requested release from immediate ties of indebtedness, eschatology might prolong the wait for release or convert literal debt into sin (e.g., Luke 12:33–34).

Petition 2 Let your kingdom come (soon) [to reorder human priorities] Q[2]

Jesus

Petition 5   [Vertical]   Release for us our debts (now),

[Horizontal] as we release our debtors (now)————————

105. Freedman and Simon, *Midrash Rabbah*, 6:840.

106. Ibid., 5:333.

107. *Mishnah Ketuboth.*

108. Freedman and Simon, *Midrash Rabbah*, 3:397.

To ask God to release debts is to ask in the name of God's rule that human oppression through debt machinations cease. Many of these machinations are abetted by the courts and other "legal" means. This leads logically into Jesus' final petition.

Petition 6 of the Second Table

Most commentators consider the sixth petition in the light of Israelite eschatology, as a request for the ultimate defeat of evil.[109] This might be close to its meaning at the Matthean or Lukan stages of redaction, but for Jesus the meaning of the sixth petition was far more mundane and pertinent to the concerns being traced up to this point. It brings into focus the subversion of justice for the weak and appeals directly to God for redress.

The Parable of the Unjust Judge (Luke 18:2–5) links nicely the situation of the lowly, issues of indebtedness, and courts of law.[110] While nothing directly states that the widow's cause pertains to debt, the word used of her unnamed adversary at law *antidikos* ("legal opponent") appears in another significant text, Luke 12:58–59 [Q]. The widow's opponent at law is likely a creditor. This picture coheres with what we previously learned about the plight typical of widows in antiquity.[111]

The twice-repeated phrase about the judge, who "neither feared God nor had respect for people" (vv. 2, 4 NRSV), offers another key linkage. The general meaning of the phrase is already suggested in 18:6 by "unjust judge," *ho kritēs tēs adikias.* Fitzmyer translates the phrase "neither feared God nor cared about human beings," citing a parallel from Josephus about King Jehoiakim, "neither reverent toward God nor fair toward human beings."[112] Irreverence captures only part of the issue. The first half of the description needs to be considered from the fact that "fear of God" for an Israelite would

109. Typical are Viviano, "The Gospel according to Matthew," 645 [42:39] at v. 13; or Stendahl, "Matthew," 778–79. Cf. Str-B. 1:422.

110. Helpful in reading this parable is Derrett, "Law in the New Testament." The parable is prefigured in Sir 35:12–18. See also Manson, *Sayings of Jesus,* 305–8.

111. And cf. Derrett, "Law in the New Testament," 187.

112. Fitzmyer, *Luke,* vol. 2, 1178

imply doing what God wants, hence, doing the will of God: From the wisdom tradition of the Old Testament comes the sentiment, "The fear of the Lord is the beginning of knowledge" (Prov 1:7). Sirach explicitly connects fear of God, God's law, and wisdom:

> The man who fears the Lord will do this,
>
> and he who holds to the law will obtain wisdom. (Sir 15:7)

It is likely, then that the judge's problem in this story, and the source of his injustice, is his lack of respect for the will of God. After all, he does not seem to take Exod 22:22 seriously.

What then might we make of the second part of this phrase, "does not regard or care for human beings"? Perhaps all that needs to be said is that this expresses in concrete form how the judge lacks fear of God. He cares not for the widow's plight. On the other hand, this is a rather bland result for such a colorful expression. There is reason to suspect some sort of idiom, undoubtedly a Semitic rather than a Greek idiom. Furthermore, we can suspect a synonymous parallelism to "not fearing God."

Some help seems afforded by a regular idiom in Old Testament Hebrew that is carried over into rabbinic usage. In the Old Testament "to lift up the face," is "to show favor, respect, or partiality to."[113] The Greek verb *entrepomai* in Luke's text also means "respect."[114] In the Old Testament showing partiality in judgment was considered heinous. "Turning one's face to silver" (i.e., accepting gifts or bribes) was thought to be synonymous with thwarting justice (Prov 6:35). In later Jewish tradition we encounter what was undoubtedly typical:

> The usual experience is: Two men go before a judge, one of them poor and the other rich; towards whom does the judge turn his face? Is it not towards the rich man?[115]

This idiom helps to understand "respect" (*entrepomai*), but the unjust judge is said *not* to show respect to human beings. Can we suspect here an ironic narrative device to emphasize the fact that the

---

113. BDB, 670; Jastrow, *Dictionary*, 937.

114. A study of the translation of the Greek verb *entrepō* in the LXX shows that on several occasions the underlying Hebrew text has an idiom involving "face" (e.g., Exod 10:3; 2 Kgs 22:19).

115. *Lev. Rab.* 3:2 (4:37).

judge *does* show partiality to the more powerful cause? Jesus' audience could then be expected to laugh (bitterly) at the judge's self-deception in Luke 18:4. Perhaps there is double meaning, too, if the judge "neither feared God nor was partial to humane considerations." He shows partiality to the powerful who can pay, but the widow has nothing to offer except her obnoxious persistence. Sirach was aware of just this sort of situation:

> Do not offer him [sc. God] a bribe, for he will not accept it . . . for the Lord is the judge, and with him is no partiality. He will not show partiality in the case of a poor man.
> . . . He will not ignore the supplications of the fatherless, nor the widow when she pours out her story. Do not the tears of the widow run down her cheek as she cries out against him who has caused them to fall? (Sir 35:12–15; cf. Prov 6:35)

If in the setting in life of Jesus the meaning of the Unjust Judge was to indict those who devour the houses of widows, then the final comment of Jesus (Luke 18:7) means something other than Luke thought (18:1). This story is not so much an example story encouraging prayer, as it is a warning to judges not to oppress the widow. Jesus promises that the God who shows great compassion for the fatherless and widow will be vindicating their cause quickly.

What then does the sixth petition mean? Its rather crude attribution of cause to God stands in good stead with previous comments about peasant sensibilities (immediacy, direct address). The *crux* of the matter has to do with the meaning of "temptation," "test" (*peirasmos*). Derived from a root *peir-*, with cognates in the Latin *experiri* and English "experience," this noun is extremely rare in non-biblical Greek.[116] Verbal forms appear with the basic senses of "to attempt" or "to put to the test." Since Homer, *peira* conveys the notion of "to test the value of something." In the Hellenistic-Roman period, the word can be associated with imperial or royal contexts in the sense of "loyalty test."[117] *Peirasmos* translates an Aramaic noun *nsiyôn* from *nssî*,

---

116. Appears only three times, BAGD, 640; Seesemann, "Πειρα," 23.

117. Egyptian papyri: Moulton and Milligan, *Vocabulary*, 501; Plutarch, *Brutus* 10.

Hebrew *nsâ*. Manifesting a field of meanings similar to the Greek *peira*, the biblical word, for instance, can refer to the testing of or attempting to use military equipment (1 Sam 17:39). Perhaps the most significant occurrence appears in biblical wisdom: Job 9:23–24 links the "trials" of the innocent (if indeed the root there is *nsâ*) with the flourishing of the wicked and the "covering of judges' faces" (i.e., the denial of justice). In later rabbinic usage, the standard understanding of "temptation" comes to the fore.[118]

Matthew's seventh petition may confirm these tentative expositions if it is seen as an editorial expansion of the meaning of Petition 6. The "evil one," then, refers to the corrupt judge who presides over a court prejudiced toward the collection of debts and rigged in favor of royal or imperial interests. The sixth and seventh petitions vividly request deliverance from subverted legal proceedings before evil judges.

In light of this discussion of the second table, it is highly probable that Jesus' Prayer originally expressed a concrete and tight-knit integrity: It is a vivid request for deliverance from hunger, debt, and trials in rigged courts before evil judges. The social system of Roman Palestine, with debt relations reinforced by temple religion, had left many hungry and marginalized. Jesus' Prayer directly addressed their plight, and held out hope that God would hear their prayer as God had heard the cry of the Israelites in Egypt.

The presence of the kingdom's power (Luke 11:20 [Q]) has profound implications for human institutions and action. Many of the parables of Jesus refer to this reordering power. It is a power as effective as yeast (Luke 13:20–21 [Q] parable of the Leaven) or a tiny seed to grow into a towering mustard shrub in a field (Mark 4:30–32 and par.). In terms of human affairs, the reign of God disorients and reorients like the sudden discovery of a priceless pearl (Matt 13:46 [Q]). The reign of God leads to surprising actions, perhaps foolish from the standpoint of conventional wisdom (the Good Samaritan, Luke 10:29–37 [L], or the Prodigal Father, Luke 15:11–32 [L]). The third petition of the first table develops this line of understanding even further.

---

118. Str-B. 1:422.

(Secondary: Petition 3 of the First Table)

The word "will" in "will of God" (*thelēma tou theou*) often translates in the Septuagint (LXX) the Hebrew word for "pleasure" of God (*ḥepeṣ*).[119] Another significant Hebrew word for "will" is *raṣôn*. In either case, the emphasis in the Semitic mind is upon the objective ethical content of God's will and its concrete performance.[120] This can be seen from a few of the Old Testament occurrences of either word:

> [The LORD] says of Cyrus, "He is my shepherd, and he shall fulfil all my *purpose*. (Isa 44:28)[121]

> The LORD loves him; he shall perform his *purpose* on Babylon . . . (Isa 48:14)[122]

> I *delight* to do thy will, O my God; thy law is within my heart. (Ps 40:8)[123]

The Psalmist brings together will and delight in the last quotation, and the parallelism between "will" and "law" is particularly noteworthy. While many of the occurrences of *ḥapaṣ* (verb) and *raṣôn* (noun) are in priestly or cultic contexts, there are also a significant number of occurrences of *ḥpṣ* (verb and noun forms) in contexts that emphasize that justice and mercy are qualities pleasing to God:

> . . . let him who glories glory in this, that he understands and knows me, that I am the Lord who practice steadfast love, justice and righteousness in the earth; for in these things I *delight*, says the LORD. (Jer 9:24)

> For I *desire* steadfast love and not sacrifice, the knowledge of God, rather than burnt offerings. (Hos 6:6)

---

119. Schrenk, "Θελημα." Cf. Shrenk, "Βουλομαι"; and McCasland, "Will of God."

120. McCasland, "Will of God."

121. "Purpose" = LXX *thelēma* = *ḥpṣ*.

122. "Purpose" = LXX *boulē* = *ḥpṣ*.

123. "Will" = LXX *thelēma* = *raṣôn*.

Perhaps the most important passages from the Old Testament for the purposes of this discussion lie in Malachi. Various words for God's pleasure or displeasure occur frequently here. Furthermore, the hope of the return of Elijah—which colors at a number of points the gospel accounts of John the Baptist's and Jesus' ministries—is brought to expression in this book. Finally, the critical stance of Malachi toward the cultus suggests some striking parallels to the Jesus traditions:

> I have no *pleasure* (*hepeṣ*) in you, says the LORD of hosts, and I will not accept an offering from your hand. (Mal 1:10)[124]

> You have wearied the LORD with your words. Yet you say, "How have we wearied him?" By saying, "Every one who does evil is good in the sight of the Lord, and he *delights* in them." (Mal 2:17)[125]

> Behold, I send my messenger . . . the messenger of the covenant in whom you *delight* . . . (Mal 3:1)[126]

> Then the offering of Judah and Jerusalem *will be pleasing* to the LORD . . . (Mal 3:4)[127]

The "will" of God, that is, what is pleasing to God, is not only cultic in Malachi, but also ethical:

> For the lips of a priest should guard knowledge, and men should seek instruction (*torah*) from his mouth, for he is the messenger of the LORD of hosts. But you have turned aside from the way; you have caused many to stumble by your instruction (*torah*); you have corrupted the covenant of Levi . . . and so I make you despised and abased before all the people, inasmuch as you have not kept my ways but have shown partiality in your instruction (*torah*). (Mal 2:7–9)

---

124. Cf. Mark 7:6–7; 12:32–34; Matt 9:13; 23:23.
125. Cf. Mark 3:4; Matt 23:27–28.
126. Cf. Mark 9:11–13; Matt 23:30, 34; Luke 4:18–19 (+ Isa 42:1).
127. Mark 11:15–19.

> I will draw near to you for judgment; I will be a swift wit-
> ness against the sorcerers, against the adulterers, against
> those who swear falsely, against those who oppress the
> hireling in his wages, the widow and the orphan, against
> those who thrust aside the sojourner, and do not fear me,
> says the LORD of hosts. (Mal 3:5)

These passages are addressed to the sons of Levi (2:8; 3:3). They
reflect ancient Israelite conceptions of the role of the Levites, who
were both cultic figures and judges rolled into one (cf. *torah*). Where
might such traditions have been preserved? Malachi is generally
dated to the early fifth century BCE—prior to the work of Nehemiah
and Ezra.[128] The nature of the criticism of the cultus evident in the
document suggests a writer among the priests, but not among the
upper echelon. In the post-exilic situation, families descended from
Aaron were the dominant figures in the Jerusalem cultus. Furthermore, the address in Malachi to the sons of Levi perhaps reveals the
interest of the author in this second-class group of priests. The book
of Ezekiel tells us that the Levites or families tracing their lineage
back to Levi had fallen into disfavor during the period immediately
after the exile (Ezek 44:10–31). Ezekiel, in fact, relates that the Aaronides, who supplant the Levites,

> shall not marry a widow, or a divorced woman . . . They
> shall teach my people the difference between the holy
> and the common, and show them how to distinguish
> between the unclean and the clean. In a controversy they
> shall act as judges, and they shall judge it according to
> my judgments. (Ezek 44:22–24)

These are the very issues that concern Malachi, so it is not entirely clear whether Malachi is thinking of the Aaronides under the
more comprehensive designation "sons of Levi." In any case, Malachi
is written from a critical, not sympathetic, point of view. The writing insists that the priests must attend both to cultic and covenantal

128. For the historical situation of Malachi, see Eissfeldt, *The Old Testament*,
442–43. Nehemiah's dates are fairly certain: 446–434 BCE. Ezra's mission has
been variously dated: The two most likely dates are 458 and 398 BCE (depend-
ing upon which Artaxerxes is meant in Ezra 7:1). Cross, "Reconstruction of the
Judean Restoration," 14 n. 60, sees 458 BCE as the more likely date. Consult
Eissfeldt, *The Old Testament*, 554–55 for the opposing arguments.

concerns. Its author is probably a lower division priest knowledge-able regarding the Old Israelite legal traditions (which combined covenant-ethical and cultic concerns). As proof of this orientation, the figure of the Old Israelite charismatic prophet, Elijah the Tish-bite, appears in the final chapters of Malachi.

The later tradition about Elijah presents fascinating material for study.[129] There are tantalizing glimpses of apparently widespread popular beliefs about Elijah. The impression given is of expectations forged in conformity with specific needs of diverse groups.

Thus, Mal 3:2 envisions the work of the Messenger (Elijah ac-cording to Mal 4:5) as "purification." Furthermore, as the passage quoted above indicates, Elijah will restore the integrity of judgment for those who are legally at a disadvantage (3:5–12). Mal 4:5 adds that Elijah will "turn the hearts" of fathers to their children. Sirach (ca. 200 BCE) adds to this list the restoration of the tribes of Israel (Sir 48:10). According to rabbinic tradition, Elijah will decide disputed questions of law.[130] On the more popular side, and reflecting tradi-tions of northern Israel, Elijah will anoint the Messiah and set up the symbols of the messianic age—the three bowls of manna, purifica-tory water, and oil.

> Thus Elijah prepares the people of God for the last time. When peace has been restored, the community reconsti-tuted, Antichrist overcome and killed and the Messiah anointed for His kingly office, then the great final age of grace begins.[131]

Elijah comes, therefore, to seal the eschatological will or plea-sure of God. The third petition of Jesus' Prayer came to evoke this matrix of expectation, and in conjunction with the other petitions to ask for the concrete observance of God's will among humankind. This point is underscored by the expansion of the third petition's probably original form in Matthew by "on earth as it is in heaven." This parallel may have been intended to go with the entire first table rather than just the third petition.[132] It certainly would be appropri-

---

129. Lightfoot, *Commentary*, 2:243–47 (*ad* Matt 17:10). Jeremias, "Ἡλ(ε)ιας," (+ bibliography). Billerbeck, "Der Prophet Elias," Appendix 28 Str-B. 4:764–98.

130. Jeremias, "Ἡλ(ε)ιας," 934.

131. Ibid.

132. Origen long ago suggested this: Smith, "Lord's Prayer," 156.

ate as an explicit conclusion to what is implied in the other petitions. Furthermore, there is latent in the third petition the intimation that those who guarantee the observance of God's will—the interpreters of the law or torah, i.e., priests, levites, scholars of Q²'s day—must come in for blame. If God's will is not now being observed as it should be, then the guarantors have failed (cf. Luke 11:52 [Q]).

This petition articulates quite concretely what is implied already in the sixth petition (and likely the seventh):

Petition 3 Let your will be done Q² [May Elijah, who judges truly, come]

Jesus

Petition 6 Do not cause us to come into a trial [court] (Matt + Luke)

Petition 7 but rescue us from the evil [judge (lit. one)] (Matt)

Originally these latter petitions articulated the immediate concerns of people threatened with foreclosure or imprisonment through court action. These sentiments were also felt to be appropriate to the agony scene in Gethsemane. There Jesus prays words quite similar to the third petition. The prayer is offered up immediately before Jesus is arrested and taken to the subverted Sanhedrin. He is being arrested precisely because he has openly criticized in his teaching (Mark 12:40) and in his actions (Mark 11:15–17) the mechanisms proliferating debt and misery in Roman Palestine around 30 CE. For Mark, Jesus is about to suffer for doing the work of Elijah.

Conclusion

The Lord's Prayer, when viewed in its original connection to the work of Jesus, displays a concrete, immediate, and consistent this-worldly concern. While we may still speak (as older scholarship does) of its basic framework of meaning as "eschatological," in the sense that it hopes for ultimate and final changes in human affairs and conditions, nevertheless, the Lord's Prayer is surprisingly more concerned with specific problems and human welfare in the here and now than might have been suspected.

This essay has argued that Jesus' original prayer consisted in the distinctive 'abba' address and Petitions 4–6; the seventh petition repeats Petition 6 in synonymous parallelism. These petitions centered around the constellation of social problems bound up with court–enforced debt collections and resulting lack of adequate bread (whether substantial, subsistence, belonging to the estate, or "daily"). The first table of the Prayer in the Q tradition elaborates on the basis of the great traditions of Israel, and reflects more abstract theological interests of these early scribes of the Jesus traditions.

The two tables of the Prayer, thus, are organically related and internally unified to a degree. Where the second table delves into specific human needs and expresses values peculiar to Jesus' Galilean movement, the first table articulates the general care of God and parameters of faithful human action. Each petition of the earlier second table correlates in some definite respect with the parallel member of the later first table:

	Table 2 *Primary (Jesus, Q^1?)*		Table 1 *Secondary (Q^2, later evangelists)*
P. 4	Petition for daily bread	P. 1	Sanctifying the name in blessing
P. 5	Request for the removal of debt	P. 2	Request for the arrival of God's kingdom
PP. 6–7	God to deliver from rigged courts and evil judges	P. 3	God's will to be done

Central to the concerns of Jesus' original Prayer was the reality of oppression, indebtedness, hunger, and social insecurity. When early Christian groups moved out of the immediate context of such social realities, the concrete and immediate meaning of Jesus' Prayer was led in the direction of theological abstractions and aligned with Israelite traditions and early rabbinic forms of prayer. Twenty-first century Christian communities might reflect on the meaning and consequences of that transition as they confront social and economic crises at the beginning of a new millennium.[133]

133. I am grateful to Jerome H. Neyrey, Dennis C. Duling, and John S. Kloppenborg for astute comments on earlier drafts of this study. They, of course, cannot be held responsible for the views promoted here.

CHAPTER 4

Jesus the Tax Resister

Whenever you enter a town and they receive you,
    eat what is set before you;
heal the sick in it and say to them,
    "The kingdom of God has come near to you." —LUKE 10:8–9 [Q[1]]

Release us from debt,
    as we release those in debt to us. —LUKE 11:3 [Q[1]]

Introduction

In chapter 3 on the Lord's Prayer, I attempted to state the original meaning of the Prayer of Jesus and trace how the concrete material concerns of Jesus became abstract theological concerns of the later scribal tradents of the Jesus material and gospels. I argued that Jesus' Prayer, presumably very closely tied to key interests behind his historical activity, articulated three concrete concerns in hunger, debt, and subverted justice. These were seen as internally related through the social situation of the early Jesus movement.

Left undone in that essay, and continued here, is a more thorough investigation of the relationship between the concrete concerns of Jesus and earliest Q. As I suggested in a 1988 article:

> literate followers of Jesus recorded and arranged his words. For these followers, whose literacy and experience

92

moved them to a greater or lesser degree out of the pre-
dominately oral culture of the countryside, the meaning
of the tradition shifted. Speaking from a different social
"place," these early [tradents] perceived the meaning of
Jesus' appearance and words in more abstract and general terms (e.g. in relationship to the destiny of the whole
people of Israel or as an appeal to the wise) . . . Yet as has
been noted by others, the Jesus tradition is one of the few
extant from antiquity where the "interface" between the
ancient expressions of the lower classes in the countryside and the records of the literate is still relatively close.[1]

Abstract theological interests surely are at work in Q^1, but this stratum of tradition is as close as we get in a consistent body of early
literary material to the historical interests and praxis of Jesus. The
situation for a critical social appraisal of Q and Jesus is now stronger
with the appearance of Kloppenborg's important book *Excavating Q*
and *The Critical Edition of Q* from the International Q Project.[2]

Furthermore, James C. Scott's comparative political studies
of peasantry are increasingly appreciated in helping to articulate
the meaning of Jesus.[3] Scott offers us a passage in *Domination and
the Arts of Resistance* that will underwrite the explorations of this
chapter:

Malay paddy farmers, in the region in which I have
conducted fieldwork, have resented paying the official
Islamic tithe. It is collected inequitably and corruptly,
the proceeds are sent to the provincial capital, and not
a single poor person in the village has even received any
charity back from the religious authorities. Quietly and
massively, the Malay peasantry has managed to nearly
dismantle the tithe system so that only 15 percent of
what is formally due is actually paid. There have been
no tithe riots, demonstrations, protests, only a patient
and effective nibbling in a multitude of ways: fraudu-
lent declarations of the amount of land farmed, simple

1. Oakman, "Rulers' Houses," 110.

2. Kloppenborg [Verbin], *Excavating Q*; Robinson, Hoffmann, and Kloppenborg, eds., *Critical Edition of Q*.

3. See Crossan, *Historical Jesus*; Crossan, *The Birth of Christianity*; Herzog,
Jesus, Justice, and the Reign of God.

failures to declare land, underpayment, and delivery of
paddy spoiled by moisture or contaminated with rocks
and mud to increase its weight.[4]

Recent Q studies and Scott's concept of peasant resistance help
us to focus on certain basic facts about the early Jesus tradition. Q
studies analyze the early sayings tradition into an earlier and a later
stratum. We get even closer to the context in which Jesus' sayings
were presumably translated from Aramaic and preserved, with at-
tendant interests. Peasant resistance (as described above by Scott)
provides a useful category to elucidate Jesus' activity.

This chapter pursues the thesis that Jesus advocated tax resistance as a concrete expression of the "kingdom of God." Jesus' historical activity attempted to facilitate the "eminent domain of God"
by brokering the remission of debts and taxes through subversive
resistance measures. He brokered remission by bringing together
tax collector and tax payer in an attempt to alleviate tax burdens, by
advocating dissimulation in representations of the tax situation (including manipulation of debt records), and by focusing his followers'
praxis through prayer for such relief. For such reasons, Jesus would
become a marked man in the eyes of the elites. The expected form of
punishment meted out to tax resisters was crucifixion. By focusing
on debts, hunger, and subverted justice, Jesus addressed in concrete
ways the fundamental power differentials of rich and poor and the
precarious livelihoods of peasants: farmers, fishers, and artisans. If
God's love, justice, and compassion was to speak to the life situations
of peasants in Galilee and Judea, these very struggles would have to
be addressed.

Jesus of Nazareth and Judas of Gamala

According to Josephus, the tax arrangements of the Roman impe-
rium implemented when Judea became a Roman province in 6 CE
were met with stiff resistance. Judas of Gamala (in Gaulanitis, the
present-day Golan Heights to the east of the Galilean lake) and a certain Zaddok the Pharisee, insisting that there is no God but God and

---

4. Scott, *Weapons of the Weak*, 89.

that paying taxes to Rome is a sign of servitude, advocated armed resistance.

> But a certain Judas, a Gaulanite from a city named Gama-la, who had enlisted the aid of Saddok, a Pharisee, threw himself into the cause of rebellion. They said that the assessment carried with it a status amounting to downright slavery, no less, and appealed to the nation to make a bid for independence. (Josephus, *Ant.* 18.4 [Feldman, LCL])

> As for the fourth of the philosophies, Judas the Galilean set himself up as leader of it. This school agrees in all other respects with the opinions of the Pharisees, except that they have a passion for liberty that is almost unconquerable, since they are convinced that God alone is their leader and master. (Josephus, *Ant.* 18.23 [Feldman, LCL])

The thesis that Jesus was a "zealot" or an armed insurrectionist, propounded by S. G. F. Brandon a generation ago, has been successfully questioned by Morton Smith, Richard Horsley, and others. However, one cannot but be struck by the proximity of Judas and Jesus, and the similarity of their messages. At the time of the census, Jesus would have been about ten years old and living only about 30 miles from Gamala. Moreover during the time of his historical activity, Jesus spent most of his time in the environs of the Galilean lake. Capernaum is within eyesight of Gamala, and vice versa.

That the central message of Jesus of Nazareth was the "kingdom of God" (in conventional translation) is among the most solidly accepted historical facts about him. The meaning of this term has been extensively debated over the years, but its similarity to the message of Judas and Zaddok has not gone unnoticed. Jesus of Nazareth was equally concerned about debt as Luke 11:3 [Q^1] shows. An examination of very early Jesus traditions will demonstrate this to be a pervasive concern. Before turning to that task, though, some words are needed about the taxation system in Roman Galilee.

The Taxation System in Roman Galilee

This section will eventually argue, though our evidence is more indirect than direct, that the client taxation system of Roman Galilee was burdensome and resented at the village level. The anti-tax sentiments of Judas attracted the notice of Josephus, a Judean writer; Josephus also mentions Jesus of Nazareth, but not in regard to taxation. One might urge, as does E. P. Sanders, that there was no taxation problem under the client rule of Herod Antipas. Sanders goes so far as to claim Antipas a "good tetrarch" and taxes at the time not "exorbitant."[5]

Obviously, the argument of this chapter depends on an understanding of the impact of taxation in early Roman Palestine. Was it light and socially innocuous, or burdensome so as become an object of resistance? Several basic approaches have been taken. Lists of taxes have been compiled, and investigations of taxes (for instance) in Josephus conducted. Such is the approach of Sanders' former student Fabian E. Udoh. After investigating "the evidence" for early Roman period taxation (especially under Pompey, Julius Caesar, Herod, and the Judean temple), Udoh can make claims such as,

> The figures which Josephus gives for the income projected for Herod's successors are, we argued, inaccurate; nor is it clear how the revenues were broken up, for instance into direct and indirect taxes. It results that in spite of the sums which Josephus gives for Herod Antipas' annual income, we still cannot determine how he raised the revenues and how the Jews in Galilee were affected by the taxes he imposed from 4 B.C.E. to circa 39 C.E. And very little can be said of taxes under the *praefecti*.[6]

Udoh is convinced that Herod the Great, Herod Antipas' father, "opened the Jewish state to opportunities" and established "economic prosperity"; further, that "Herod's taxes were not as ruinous to his kingdom as is usually assumed."[7] Udoh in this follows the general lines of Sanders. He concludes that taxation levels and economic factors do not account for political developments in early Roman Palestine; these are left to vaguely specified ideological and political factors.

The older approach to taxation of Frederick C. Grant remains influential. Grant saw two competing tax systems up to 70 CE in

---

5. Sanders, *The Historical Figure of Jesus*, 21.

6. Udoh, "Tribute and Taxes in Early Roman Palestine," 335.

7. Ibid., 336.

Roman Palestine—the imperial and the temple. Since these operated somewhat independently, Grant saw their net effect as burdensome.[8]

Neither of these approaches incorporates the results of comparative social science. Studies of Lenski, Kautsky, and Sjøberg have been very influential lately in rethinking the social impact of taxation in agrarian contexts. Lists cannot begin to elucidate the social dynamics of agrarian taxation; competing social groups gets us closer to the truth. In my doctoral dissertation I incorporated such comparative perspectives, in addition to Eric Wolf's notions about the impact of exactions on peasant subsistence, to see a cultivator living on the edge. Subsistence and consumption needs were endangered in early Roman Palestine, and the appearance of overt revolts (4 BCE, 6 CE, 66 CE) and banditry corroborates. What lists and competing systems (of factions) cannot show, though, is the positive feedback arrangement of agrarian tax systems. (Positive and negative feedback are terms from Systems Theory. Positive feedback amplifies; negative feedback attenuates.) Such tax systems do not have checks and balances to protect the cultivator.

Methodologically, a simple model will illustrate:

Figure 4.1: System of Taxation in Roman Palestine

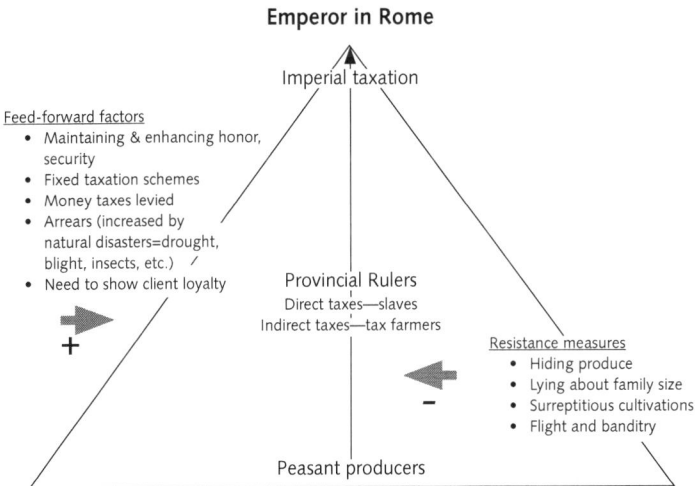

Emperor in Rome

Imperial taxation

Feed-forward factors
- Maintaining & enhancing honor, security
- Fixed taxation schemes
- Money taxes levied
- Arrears (increased by natural disasters=drought, blight, insects, etc.)
- Need to show client loyalty

+

Provincial Rulers
Direct taxes—slaves
Indirect taxes—tax farmers

Resistance measures
- Hiding produce
- Lying about family size
- Surreptitious cultivations
- Flight and banditry

−

Peasant producers

---

8. Grant, *Economic Background of the Gospels*.

BRIEF EXPLANATION OF THE DIAGRAM:

Provincial elites (e.g, the Herodian rulers) must meet imperial demands for produce as well as demonstrate client loyalty; patron–client relations levy significant burdens (Augustus–Herod the Great); direct taxes collected by slaves (*oikonomoi*), indirect taxes collected through tax-farming arrangements (*telōnai*). While the Q tradents were likely village scribes (*kōmogrammateis*, see below), their association with the tax collection social stratum deeply reflects that ethos.

Early imperial taxes were fixed and levied in imperial silver. These were exacted from an agricultural base, hence had to be "converted" from in kind to in specie [i.e., in coin]. Fixed or invariable taxes showed no respect for natural variance in product. Arrears or tax debt were tabulated in written records kept in royal and imperial archives.

Peasants had a number of means of ordinary resistance, though none of these did away with the systemic problem. Revolts were few and far between because of the perennial localism of peasants and the highly organized means of violence in the hands of elite groups. Not surprisingly, the Judean Revolt of 66–70 CE was accompanied by tax remedies.

Jesus' Associations with "Tax Collectors and Sinners"

A significant datum about Jesus of Nazareth in the early material of the Synoptic Gospels is his association with "tax collectors and sinners" (Q both strata, and Mark). The word "tax collector" (*telōnēs*) appears absolutely only in M and L—the materials unique to Matthew and Luke, respectively (Matt 10:3; Luke 3:12; 7:29[Q?]; 18:10, 11, 13; 19:2 "chief tax collector"). Otherwise, the word is paired with other words: "sinners" (*hamartōloi*; Luke 7:34 [Q²]; Mark 2:15; Luke 15:2 [L]), "Gentiles" (*ethnikoi*; Luke 6:34 [Q] and Matt 5:46-47 [Q]; Matt 18:17 [M]; see Q¹: Luke 6:34 and Matt 5:46-47 [Q]), "prostitutes" (*pornai,* Matt 21:31–32 [M], or "adulterers" (*moichoi,* Luke 18:11 [L]). John Donahue thus can summarize: "The word is never found outside the Synoptic Gospels and, in them, only in the pre-Jerusalem setting of Jesus' ministry, usually in the framework of controversy stories. Thus from a source critical viewpoint, 'toll collectors and sinners,' is found as a set phrase in Mark and Q."[9]

Although this association might be evaluated as "literary invention" or invective by opponents, the criterion of embarrassment would argue against both (since it would be difficult to imagine why the early tradents would invent or preserve this material).[10] Kloppenborg's observations about the locus of early Q as "wisdom" give significant reason for considering this information as positive historical data:

> If one asks, who would be in a position to frame the Sayings Gospel as it has been framed, the answer would appear to be village and town notaries and scribes . . . There is ample evidence from Egypt to indicate the presence of a variety of scribes, of varying educational levels, in towns and villages, some serving in the apparatus of the provincial administration and others functioning as freelance professionals. The *kōmogrammateus* (village scribe) was concerned with tax and census matters.[11]

What has not happened yet given this insight is a move toward the political significance of this association. As Kloppenborg's own discussion of recent Q scholarship testifies, most interpretations of the material depend upon assumptions about their alleged philosophical or religious concern.[12] The following commentary explores the

9. Donahue, "Tax Collectors and Sinners," 55.

10. On tax collector (*telōnēs*) as a stock term in invective, see MacMullen, *Roman Social Relations,* Appendix B, "The Lexicon of Snobbery." The criterion of embarrassment, one of the standard criteria in the historical criticism of the gospels, urges that it is very unlikely that some embarrassing detail in the tradition has been invented or inserted later. For example, it is unlikely that Jesus' crucifixion was invented because it was a most shameful death. The earliest New Testament witness Paul attests its shamefulness for an honor–shame culture in Gal 3:13; 1 Cor 1:18, 27; and elsewhere.

11. Kloppenborg, *Excavating Q,* 200–201.

12. Ibid., 166–213. Kloppenborg and Piper have moved the discussion in a more social direction.

significance in a very different direction. For one must ask why Jesus associated as of central concern with village scribes, "tax collectors," and "sinners."

Jesus was attempting to mitigate the situation of the indebted ("sinner") by promoting the subversion of the imperial tax system in Galilee. This subversion would have operated both in terms of tax evasion and distortion of the tax records.

Earliest Q Recension: What the Tax Collectors Heard

This selective commentary on Q material limits itself to Kloppenborg's Q¹ stratum, though parts are jettisoned to concord with the new critical text of Q.[13] At the end, "resonances" in other early Jesus traditions are also noted.

As I have argued, Q¹ perhaps began to be set down in Jesus' own lifetime, by scribal groups around the Lake of Galilee associated with the Tiberian archives. These were transferred back to Sepphoris under Agrippa II (ca. 54 CE); hence, Q² represents a "Judean recension" of Q incorporating prophetic and Deuteronomic interests of scribes hostile to the temple and Pharisees.[14] Q¹ is notably distant from Judean issues, and more directly concerned with the political situation under Antipas.

The First Early Q Discourse:
God's Patronage as Liberating Eminent Domain

The first sayings collection of early Q reflects on the ethos and largesse of God's eminent domain. With roots in Passover meditation, and perhaps the example of Moses in mind (Exod 2:11–12), these sayings inculcate a wisdom of higher liberative purpose.

---

13. Our mini-commentary depends on Kloppenborg's analysis of Q¹ in *The Formation of Q*, Appendix 2. Translations are usually the NRSV with slight modifications in light of the Greek text of Luke; Luke's text is usually more elaborated in contrast to reconstructed Q in Robinson, Hoffmann, and Kloppenborg, eds., *Critical Edition of Q*. The standard procedure is to cite Q according to the Lukan location (with a few exceptions from Matthew).

14. Pages 43–55 above.

Luke 6:20b–23

How honorable are you poor,
for yours is the kingdom of God.
How honorable are you who are hungry now,
for you shall be filled.
How honorable are you who weep now,
for you will laugh.
How honorable are you when people hate you,
and when they exclude you, revile you, and defame you
on account of the Son of Man.
Rejoice in that day and leap for joy,
for that is what their ancestors did to the prophets.

I have argued elsewhere that these words allude to some form of the first-century Passover Haggadah.[15] Thus, they bespeak a concern at the beginning of the very earliest Jesus material a concern for liberation in the Mosaic mold. They also corroborate the connection made between Jesus of Nazareth and Judas of Gamala.

Luke 6:27–28

Love your enemies,
do good to those who hate you,
bless those who curse you,
pray for those who abuse you.

Early Q immediately takes up the theme "love for enemies." A series of four descriptors is given. These descriptors indicate severely conflictual relations as would obtain when the tax collector appears. Regarding "abuse," cf. 1 Pet 3:16; Josephus, *Ant.* 16.160, 170. In this passage from Josephus, Judeans of Cyrene complain to Marcus

---

15. Most extensively in Oakman, "Models and Archaeology in the Social Interpretation of Jesus," 128–31. The first two sayings appear separately in *Gospel of Thomas* 54 and 69b, and the *Gospel of Thomas* has no parallel to the third saying. While it could be argued that the Q tradents have provided the conjunction of the sayings, they are much closer to the original context of meaning. Thus in my view, the sphere of meaning provided by Israelite tradition and Judas of Gamala is much more salient. The *Thomas* tradents, whether in Syria or Egypt, were clearly not interested in Passover connections.

Agrippa "that they are abused by certain informers, and, under pretense of taxes which were not due, are hindered from sending them."

Luke 6:29–30

If anyone strike you on the cheek,
offer the other also;
and from anyone who takes away your coat
do not withhold even your shirt.
Give to everyone who begs from you;
and if anyone takes away your goods,
do not ask for them again.

Nonretaliation for a dishonorable slap to the cheek, permitting the seizure of both outer- and under-garments indicate a quite different set of relations between tax collector and tax payer. No longer are goods seized in the name of the Galilean Crown, but now goods are redistributed in the name of God's eminent domain.

Matthew 5:41 [Possibly Q]

And if anyone forces you to go one mile,
go also the second mile.

The appearance of the important word "force" (*angareuo*) deserves comment. This was the word regularly used in the Roman East (with roots back into the Hellenistic period, as shown by Josephus, *Ant.* 13.52 and the Egyptian papyri) to denote service compelled by the Crown. This compulsion is really a form of labor taxation! The doubling of the service is an acted parable of God's eminent domain.

Luke 6:31

Do to others as you would have them do to you.

The "Golden Rule" is not stated here as a generalized ethical norm, but as a reversal of the normal dynamics of imperial taxation. In other words, Jesus' word in context had a much more limited scope of urging the subversion or reversal of the usual direction of imperial taxation.

Luke 6:32

If you love those who love you, what credit is that to you?
For even sinners love those who love them.

The interpretation of this saying hinges on the meaning of "sinners" (*hamartōloi*). To put the matter as clearly as possible, the word is usually understood to refer to those whose relations with God are disordered either through impurity or ethical infraction. Matthew Black and others, however, long ago called attention to the ambiguity of the Aramaic term *ḥôbâ*.[16] As a translation of the Aramaic *ḥôbayin*, the word could just as well refer to the condition of those in irretrievable indebtedness. Matthew's "tax collectors" is surely redactional (shifting the meaning in the direction of moral and theological disorder); however, tax collectors were also in debt and so "sinners" could be understood to refer generally to "those indebted." Given this understanding, the saying sharply highlights the ordinariness of conventional morality when even the indebted practice balanced reciprocity. In other words, there is no "moral credit" from the careful accounting and repayment of debts (balanced reciprocity), but there is moral credit in God's eyes with loans that are not expected to be repaid. God's eminent domain will call forth a more radical ethic commensurate with debt- and tax-forgiveness.

Luke 6:34 [Probably Q]

If you lend to those from whom you hope to receive,
what credit is that to you?
Even sinners lend to sinners,
to receive as much again.

The subjunctive "[if] you lend" has in view the handling of money loans. This would be the prerogative of someone in elite

---

16. Black, *An Aramaic Approach*, 140.

circumstances, or perhaps of a moneychanger ("banker," the main role of whom was to exchange politically weak coinage into authorized coinage). Concessions to change money were farmed, hence could fall into the realm of the tax collectors.

Luke 6:36–(38)

> Be merciful,
>> just as your Father is merciful.
> Do not judge,
>> and you will not be judged;
> do not condemn,
>> and you will not be condemned.
> Forgive,
>> and you will be forgiven;
> give,
>> and it will be given to you . . .
> For the measure you give
>> will be the measure you get back.

"Mercy" is practiced specifically as "Do not judge, and you will not be judged." The steward and tax collector are not to execute against the debtor. The aphorism about measuring resonates within the framework of in-kind taxation.

The Second Early Q Discourse:
The Praxis of God's Eminent Domain

The so-called "Mission Discourse" is almost universally discussed as though it were a description of either wandering itinerants or cynic-like missionaries of the Jesus movement. In other words, this sayings collection is treated as though it were "religious" or "philosophical," in line with the ideology of high imperial culture. These sayings assume a quite different aspect when they are understood to reflect the tax-resistance praxis of Jesus!

The sayings about "following" take up the implications of movements and action in the name of the Crown.

Luke 9:58

> Foxes have holes,
>> and birds of the air have nests;
> but the son of man has nowhere to lay his head.

These words reflect the life of the elites at Sepphoris (Aram. *ṣipôrîn* = birds) with their extensive storehouses, and appeal to the stewards and tax collectors to take pity on the landless commoner ("son of man").[17]

Luke 9:59–60

> To another he said, "Follow me."
>> But he said, "Lord, first let me go and bury my father."
> But Jesus said to him, "Let the dead bury their own dead;
>> but as for you, go and proclaim the kingdom of God."

The image is one of hyperbole, but reflects the social disruption of the Crown's compulsory demands. "The dead," whether literally or figuratively as the ruling elite, will take care of themselves, but the need for tax relief is pressing. Like other sayings of Jesus, this is not a literal description of his "discipleship," but a sarcastic characterization of his social circumstances (cf. Luke 19:26 [Q²]).[18]

Luke 10:2

> The harvest is plentiful,
>> but the laborers are few;

17. "Son of the Man" as a throne rival: Oakman, "Rulers' Houses, Thieves, and Usurpers," 117; Sepphoris: "Models and Archaeology in the Social Interpretation of Jesus," 120: "Jesus is said to refer to Herod as 'that fox' (Luke 13:31–33); Sepphoris derives from the Hebrew word for bird. The natural image now receives a natural political referent: The 'birds of the air,' the Sepphoreans, control the villages and the product of the land. Such a reference to the elite receives support when one considers a saying of Tiberius Gracchus (Plutarch, *Tiberius Gracchus* 9.1)—a point first noticed by Arnold Toynbee (Brown, 'Prometheus, the Servant of Yahweh, Jesus,' 113)."

18. Judean burial practices involved time-consuming waits (for secondary burials, where after the flesh decayed the bones of the deceased were relocated to be with other deceased family members, up to a year); see McCane, "Let the Dead Bury Their Own Dead."

therefore ask the lord of the harvest
    to send out laborers into his harvest.

Irony continues in this statement. "The laborers" and "the lord" refer not to religious missionaries of God, but to the customary tax collectors and the Crown. Irony comes in because Jesus and his audience know that the laborers now operate under the eminent domain of God to make sure more of the harvest remains in the village and the Crown is deprived of its due.

Luke 10:3

Go on your way.
See, I am sending you out like lambs
    into the midst of wolves.

In a reversal of the expected image (tax-payers are the sheep fleeced by the wolves), the tax collectors supporting Jesus' cause and praxis are the ones in danger.

Luke 10:4 [& Matt 10:10]

Carry no purse, no bag, no sandals, [nor staff];
    and greet no one on the road.

Would tax collectors literally have traveled this way in their official capacities? A staff is associated with tax collectors. As this text could also allude to a Passover liturgy (see *Ezek. Trag.* 181–184), it reminds that the praxis is liberative in the same way that the Israelites departed Egypt. The tax collectors give up their customary demands in a symbolic exodus from their imperial role.

Luke 10:5–6

Whatever house you enter, first say,
    "Peace to this house!"
And if anyone who shares in your peace,
    your peace will rest on that person;

> *but if not,*
> *it will return to you.*

"Entry into a house" has the appearance of the customary intrusive access of the tax collector. Verb forms for "enter" (*eperchomai* and *epeiserchomai*) appear in the Egyptian papyri in conjunction with forced entry by tax collectors. The Talmud also uses the phrase "entry of a house" regularly in this connection.[19] The greeting of peace may reflect customary practices (with extreme irony again intended), but in this context suggests subversively the surprise that comes with God's eminent domain. The householder may not accept the "peace," not wanting to run the risk of punishment for tax evasion, which probably means that the tax collector has to play the usual coercive role.

Luke 10:7–8

> *Remain in the same house,*
>   *eating and drinking whatever they provide,*
>   *for the laborer deserves to be paid.*
> *Do not move about from house to house.*
> *Whenever you enter a town*
>   *and its people welcome you,*
>   *eat what is set before you.*

But if the envoy is accepted and fed, and the tax and debt remissions are effected (God's patronage), no additional exactions are to be requested or accepted (see Luke 3:13). A conventional proverb endorses these arrangements (v. 7).

Luke 10:9

> *Heal the sick who are there, and say to them,*
>   *"The kingdom of God has come near to you."*

Just as the tax collectors metaphorically are "laborers," so also metaphorically are they "physicians." They heal by reducing the tax load

19. Donahue, "Tax Collectors and Sinners," 50, lists examples from *m. Ṭehar.* 7:6 and *m. Ḥag.* 3:6.

and ease the pressure against the subsistence margin. Hence, their "medical practice" is an expression of God's eminent domain (v. 9b).

The Third Early Q Discourse:
God's Patronage and Debt Remission

Luke 11:2–4

When you pray, say:
Father,
may your name be sanctified,
may your kingdom come.
Give us today our daily bread.
And forgive us our debts,
as we ourselves forgive everyone indebted to us.
And do not bring us to the time of trial.

The conclusions of chapter 3 regarding the Prayer of Jesus have already been indicated. However, they are modified slightly in this connection. Perhaps the most convincing evidence for this chapter's thesis is found in Luke 11:3 [Q]. For now, the petition is resonant in other ways:

Release us (tax collectors) *from debt,*
as we release those in debt to us (those who owe taxes).

Who would have collected taxes? Would such people have done this willingly? Direct taxes were gathered by slaves or agents of the responsible provincial elites. Farmed taxes (e.g., tolls) were apparently collected by the "free," but these people were indebted (provided sureties) for the amount. We know of three prominent tax collectors in early Roman Palestine: John of Caesarea, John of Gischala, and Bar Mayan. An interesting comparative instance from Pompeii:

Holograph [acknowledgment] of Privatus, public slave of the colony of Veneria Cornelia, on receipt of 1,652 sesterces for the fullers' tax of the first year . . . I, Privatus, slave of the colony, hereby declare in writing that I

received from Lucius Caecilius Jucundus 1,652 sesterces
for the fullers' tax from the balance of the first year.[20]

A municipal tax has been farmed to Jucundus, who provides col-
lateral for the tax and pays it in installments. The collection is done
by the slave Privatus. The roles of the imperial tax-collection systems
are occupied by people under various forms of compulsion.

Luke 11:9–10

Ask, and it will be given you;
   search, and you will find;
   knock, and the door will be opened for you.
For everyone who asks receives,
   and everyone who searches finds,
   and for everyone who knocks, the door will be opened.

"Asking," "searching," and "knocking" are activities related to on-site
evaluation of the tax situation.

Luke 11:11–13 [& Matt 7:11]

Is there anyone among you who,
   if your child asks for a fish,
   will give a snake instead of a fish?
Or if the child asks for an egg,
   will give a scorpion?
If you then, who are evil,
   know how to give good gifts to your children,
how much more will the heavenly Father give
   [good things] to those who ask him!

These rhetorical questions illuminate the situation of need for the village tax payer. They do not need a written tax receipt, or money, but
real consumption goods. As I have argued in previous work, peasants
cannot eat a token [coinage], but require real goods.[21]

20. *CIL* 4: 3,340, cxli, quoted in Lewis and Reinhold, ed., *Roman Civilization*, vol. 2, 333.

21. Oakman, *Jesus and the Peasants*, chap. 7: "Money in the Moral Universe

The Fourth Early Q Discourse:
Fearless Action and the Danger of Delation

Rostovtzeff comments on the frequency during the Hellenistic period of those who turn in royal opponents (including tax evaders):

> [In Ecclesiastes, under Ptolemy II] The spies of Ptolemy, who are so ubiquitous that "a bird of the air shall carry the voice" of him who cursed the king in secret, were presumably both fiscal and political *mēnutai*.[22]

The same pattern continued into the Roman period with the phenomenon of *delatio* (the act of informing the authorities about political crimes). Irony again frames the following Q-words (with God's eminent domain finessing Herod's royal or Roman imperial prerogatives).

Luke 12:2–3

Nothing is covered up that will not be uncovered,
and nothing secret that will not be known.

Nothing can remain secret. Relating to tax collection, all tax records will be open books: who has paid, who has not, and who has been abusive in confiscation.

Luke 12:4–5

I tell you, my friends,
do not fear those who kill the body,
*   and after that can do nothing more.*
But I will warn you whom to fear:
*   fear him who, after he has killed,*
*   has authority to cast into hell [Gehenna].*
Yes, I tell you, fear him!

---

of the New Testament."

22. Rostovtzeff, *SEHHW*, 350.

So there is no need to fear. The authorities only have power over the individual body, but not the resistance movement's power.

Luke 12:6–7

Are not five sparrows sold for two copper coins?
Yet not one of them is forgotten in God's sight.

Nothing gets sold in the market without the Sovereign's knowledge. All is subject to the tax! God's observation and accounting is even more rigorous than the taxation system.

Luke 12:11–12

When they bring you
before the synagogues, the rulers, and the authorities,
do not worry about how you are to defend yourselves
or what you are to say;
for the Holy Spirit will teach you
at that very hour what you ought to say.

The synagogue here is the place of public assembly and examination. The hippodrome at Tarichaeae can play a similar function when Josephus is accused of treason by Jesus son of Sapphias, the chief magistrate of Tiberias (*Life* 132). Josephus addresses assemblies at the stadium in Tiberias (*Life* 92, 331).

The Fifth Early Q Discourse:
God's Patronage and Subsistence Anxiety

Subsistence security is tied to "seeking first God's eminent domain" (Luke 12:31 [Q]). A selection of concerns related to our theme is highlighted here.

Luke 12:24

Consider the ravens:
they neither sow nor reap,

they have neither storehouse nor barn,
*   and yet God feeds them.*
Of how much more value are you than the birds.

The storehouse economy is contrasted now with the economy of the kingdom. The birds recall those of 12:6–7 (objects of royal/imperial taxation) and 9:58 (allegorically, the elites of Sepphoris), but these now are enemies of the sown. They steal from the crown as expression of God's eminent domain. Even more than thieving ravens, Jesus' associates stand to benefit from the scheme of the kingdom. Tax-resistance pays!

Luke 12:27

Consider the lilies, how they grow,
*   they neither toil nor spin;*
yet I tell you, even Solomon in all his glory
*   was not clothed like one of these.*

The "lilies" are weeds, again proliferating against the sown.[23] Just as weeds thrive amidst the sown, in this case the poppies amidst the royal wheat of Palestine, Jesus sees allegorically the success of a subversive tax-resistance.

The Sixth Early Q Discourse:
How Difficult for the Powerful-Rich to Enter God's Domain

Early Q ends with a warning that underscores the difficulty of Jesus' praxis for the powerful-rich and for those concerned about family.

Luke 13:24

Strive to enter through the narrow door;
*   for many, I tell you, will try to enter and will not be able.*

23. In earlier work, I discussed these plant images as drawing an analogy between weeds and the power of the kingdom; see Oakman, "Social Meaning and Rural Context." This is a new application of that idea.

The narrow gate is difficult of access. Such is Jesus' praxis. Is there a palace image here, suggestive of privileged access? Mark 10:25 makes a similar point. Matthew expands the saying in the direction of the conventional two ways of wisdom.

Luke 14:26

Whoever comes to me
    and does not hate
father and mother,
    wife and children,
brothers and sisters,
    yes, and even life itself,
cannot be my disciple.

Hatred of family members (understood ironically) implies that one's actions for the sake of God's eminent domain put family members at grave risk. Besides the implications of Matt 18:25, there is the story told by Philo about the actions of an Egyptian tax collector:

> Recently a man was appointed tax collector among us. When some of those who were supposed to owe taxes fled because of poverty and in fear of unbearable punishment, he carried off by force their wives, their children, the parents, and the rest of their families, striking them, and insulting them, and visiting all manner of outrages upon them in an effort to force them either to inform against the fugitive or else to make payment in his stead.[24]

Luke 14:27

Whoever does not bear his own cross and come after me,
    cannot be my disciple.

This saying provides the crux of the whole argument. For it indicates very clearly Jesus' consciousness of the political consequences deriving from his praxis (see next section). The presence of this saying

24. Philo, *Spec. Laws* 2.19.92–94, quoted in Lewis and Reinhold, ed., *The Empire*, vol. 2, 400.

can hardly be understood as an invention of the Q tradents (who say hardly a word otherwise about Jesus' death). If it is hyperbole, why would it be associated with family and bodily danger? The saying's literal meaning must then be taken seriously on the very lips of Jesus. In other words, to follow Jesus' program of tax resistance and siding with the peasants and impoverished against the Crown and its elites may involve real danger to life, limb, and family.

Luke 17:33

Whoever seeks to gain his life will lose it,
but whoever loses his life will preserve it.

Recalls Q 12:31.

Luke 14:34–35

Salt is good;
but if salt has lost its usefulness,
how shall its saltiness be restored?
It is fit neither for the land nor for the dunghill;
men throw it away.

The final image is from the simple courtyard oven. It cannot be fired without the catalyst of salt as an inner lining.[25] Just so, God's eminent domain, the "oven," will not fire without the catalyst, praxis such as Jesus': see Luke 12:28 (Q^1). The image of fire gets taken further in Luke 3:9; 12:49 (both Q^2).

Evidence from Other Early Jesus Material

Interesting corroborations of these interpretations are found in other good early Jesus material. Here only a few instances are reviewed.

---

25. Pilch, *The Cultural Dictionary of the Bible*, 4–5.

Matthew 18:34 [M]

And in anger, his lord delivered him to the jailers,
till he should pay all his debt.

The remission of enormous tax debt here is noteworthy. The slaves are expected to follow suit.[26]

Luke 16:1–8 [Q²]

He also said to the disciples, "There was a rich man who had a manager, and charges were brought to him that this man was squandering his property. So he summoned him and said to him, 'What is this that I hear about you? Give me an accounting of your management, because you cannot be my manager any longer.' then the manager said to himself, 'What will I do, now that my master is taking the position away from me? I am not strong enough to dig, and I am ashamed to beg. I have decided what to do so that, when I am dismissed as manager, people may welcome me into their homes.' So, summoning his master's debtors one by one, he asked the first, 'How much do you owe my master?' He answered, 'A hundred jugs of olive oil.' He said to him, 'Take your bill, sit down quickly, and make it fifty.' Then he asked another, 'And how much do you owe?' He replied, 'A hundred containers of wheat.' He said to him, 'Take your bill and make it eighty.' And his master commended the dishonest manager because he had acted shrewdly; for the children of this age are more shrewd in dealing with their own generation than are the children of light.

In a very different light, now, the political significance of this parable lies open for scrutiny. A steward manipulates debt (tax?) records in his own interests and against those of the master. These manipulations are viewed positively (v. 8), and the steward anticipates "being welcomed into their [villagers'] houses."

---

26. See the discussion in chapter 2.

Whether Mark 12:17 ("Give to the emperor the things that are the emperor's, and to God the things that are God's") might be invoked in support of the argument is debatable, though it shows the liveliness and danger of the tax question. Evidence may be selectively preserved even at the level of the evangelists, since in Luke 23:2 Jesus is accused before Pilate of advocating tax evasion ("We found this man perverting our nation, forbidding us to pay taxes to the emperor"). The Matt 17:26b [M] saying ("The children are free") is also noteworthy.

Jesus' Death as a Bandit

The fact of Jesus' crucifixion is the most certain historical datum we have. Q, of course, is silent about Jesus' death, but Mark reports that Jesus was crucified with two other bandits (*lēstai*). The cross was the Roman punishment reserved for seditious provincials.

Tacitus, *Annals* 1.72–73: "Tiberius gave new impetus to the law of treason. This law had the same name in olden times, but other matters came under its jurisdiction—betrayal of an army, or inciting the plebs to sedition, in short, any public malfeasance which diminished the majesty of the Roman people."[27]

Justinian's *Digest* indicates that these actions were considered treasonable: "men are gathered together for seditious purposes . . . a person . . . knowingly makes or cites a false entry in the public records . . . Moreover, the Julian Law on Treason directs that a person who injures the majesty of the state is liable to prosecution . . . by whom with malice aforethought anyone is bound by oath to act against the state . . . if a person is accused of treason under any other section of the Julian Law, his death extinguishes the charge."[28]

Paulus, *Opinions* 5.22–24, indicates disposition in capital crimes (though only Roman citizens receive "capital punishment," i.e. decapitation): "Instigators of sedition and riot or rousers of the people are, according to the nature of their rank, either crucified,

---

27. Quoted in Lewis and Reinhold, *The Empire*, 93.

28. Ibid., 30.

thrown to wild beasts, or deported to an island . . . humble persons
. . . are either crucified or thrown to wild beasts."[29]

All of this gives historical basis for asserting that Jesus of Nazareth suffered crucifixion ca. 30 CE for crimes against the majesty of
the Roman people (*crimen maiestatis Romanorum*, viz. as this chapter has argued, for conspiring to subvert the Roman taxation system
within the client realm of Herod Antipas).

Conclusion: The Meaning of Resistance
and the Resistivity of Meaning in the Jesus Traditions

The activity of historical Jesus, reflected not only in earliest Q but
also in other important Jesus materials, signified tax subversion in
the name of the eminent domain of God's ruling power. The meaning
of Jesus' resistance has not been obliterated by later scribal interests
in the gospels, so the resistivity of meaning is a noteworthy feature
in the tradition (given prevelant postmodern suspicions about such
historical judgments).

Jesus' historical activity was essentially about politics, and the
restructuring of society, and not about religion or theology. Jesus
was a conservative in relation to the traditions of Israel; like Judas
of Gamala, Jesus accepted the basic themes of Exodus in the Israelite
Scriptures. Both men applied their understandings to the concrete
social problems of their Golan/Galilean context. Judas and Zadok,
however, advocated violent resistance to Rome; Jesus was not a fol-
lower of the Fourth Philosophy in that respect. But he agreed with the
Fourth Philosophy regarding the eminent domain of God, its implications for tax resistance, and the servile condition of indebtedness.

Clarity about this result can only come with the aid of the social
sciences. This is not "reductionism," if by that is meant an obliteration
of Jesus' on-going significance; rather, this result represents a clarity
about the deepest historical significance of Jesus' work—tied as it was
to the interests of the little people and their subsistence ethic. To continue to discuss the meaning of historical Jesus in terms of German
idealism or anachronistic Euro-American experience runs the danger of great historic obfuscation. While Jesus' historical resistance to

29. Ibid., 548.

imperial and colonial realities left its traces in his traditions, it is also true that the canonical gospels of the New Testament shifted Jesus' focus from social relations to relations between human beings and God. In this sense, the New Testament made an early contribution to obscuring the meaning of Jesus' resistance.

Conclusion

Need or Greed as the Proper End of Economics?

If there is among you anyone in need, a member of your community
in any of your towns within the land that the LORD your God is giving
you, do not be hard-hearted or tight-fisted toward your needy neighbor. You should rather open your hand, willingly lending enough to
meet the need, whatever it may be.

—DEUTERONOMY 15:7–8

Financial indebtedness often originates out of need, but financial in-
vestments under global capitalism are more often in service of greed.
The foregoing chapters have investigated a deepseated concern in
Jesus of Nazareth for the alleviation of enervating debt and the satis-
faction of human need. With this concern, he showed resonance with
one of the great themes of the Bible—economic justice.[1]

The legal traditions of Israel in Deuteronomy and Leviticus
reveal the interests and stress points of Israelite "commoner economics." Deuteronomy 24:6 concerns the seriousness of taking a
millstone (for grinding grain) in pledge, "for that would be taking a

---

1. For an excellent recent treatment of economic themes in the Bible, see
now Barrera, *Biblical Economic Ethics*. This book is especially valuable because
Barrera holds doctorates in both economics and biblical studies. See the Graeber quote in the Preface (p. xiv above).

life in pledge." Compare Sirach, who writes (34:24), "The bread of the needy is the life of the poor; whoever deprives them of it is a murderer." Deuteronomy 24:10–13 show that clothing taken in pledge for loans are strictly to be short-term so as not to deny the debtor use of a necessity. Wages are to be paid by the day (24:14–15). Aliens, orphans, and widows are not to be denied justice (24:17–18). And left-overs from the harvests of grain, grapes, olives, are to be left to be gleaned by alien, orphan, widow (24:19–22). The Deuteronomists remind Israel that this accords with their own liberation from slavery in Egypt (24:22).

For all of this, Deut 15:7 acknowledges that there will be those in need (in great tension with 15:4 "there will, however, be no one in need"). The provision for debt release every seven years (Deut 15:1) indicates the prevalence of the problem of agrarian debt and the attempt of levitical law to remediate it. In the ancient world, the revolutionary cry of peasants was often debt-release and land redistribution.[2] That these two problems—debt and denial of land access—threaten peasant subsistence is easily understood. Land and labor are the only factors of production fundamentally relevant to the peasant producer, and labor is the only factor really under the producer's control. Not surprisingly, the Priestly law in Leviticus addresses both debt and land with the idealistic Jubilee legislation. The Jubilee envisions land redistribution and redemption from debt slavery (Lev 25:10, 13, 25, 41); however, foreign slaves are not accorded this liberation (25:44–46). This legislation is clearly for insiders only!

This tradition of concern for "Israelite commoners" is sustained with Jesus of Nazareth. Jesus obtained a reputation as an effective broker of the kingdom of God, through his ability to connect those in need with those in possession.[3] This could be food or debt relief (Q/ Luke 11:3–4). His politics consequently were focused upon adequate subsistence and the tyranny of Mammon (Q/Luke 6:20–21; L/Luke 12:16–21; Q/Luke 16:13; see Sir 5:1, 8). While Jesus can speak with sympathy about the traveling Samaritan, he does not appear to have appreciated commerce or commercialization (Q/Luke 19:12–26;

---

2. Oakman, *The Political Aims of Jesus*, 102.

3. Ibid., 70.

GThom 64). In agrarian settings, commercial agriculture or trade can provide capital that further indentures the ordinary producer.

Robert Bellah, discussing the work of Max Weber, suggests the insight that the ethic of Jesus had upended the norm of "love family and friends–do harm to enemies" by erasing the boundary between family and stranger (L/Luke 10:30–35) and offering generalized reciprocity to strangers (Q/Luke 6:32–36). Bellah writes, "What has happened to the two principles of the ancient ethic of neighborliness is that the principle of the contrast between in-group and out-group has been abandoned and the principle of reciprocity has been absolutized."[4]

Ironically, with the transition of the message about Jesus from Syro-Palestine to the major cities of the eastern Roman Empire, the carriers of the Christian message become traveling tradesmen and commercial people. Transformations of economic attitudes within the movement can be traced in part with respect to money: While Jesus made God and Mammon (money on loan or deposit, the estate storehouse) a strict either/or, the later New Testament writers simply warn against the "love of money" (1 Tim 3:3; 6:10; 2 Tim 3:2; Heb 13:5; see Luke 16:14 and Eccl 5:10). After all, they have to deal with money in the regular course of business.[5] For all of this, the writer of Acts could claim that the Jerusalem Jesus-followers held everything in common (Acts 2:44–45; 4:32–35), and that the one word of Jesus in the New Testament outside of the gospels is "It is more blessed to give than to receive" (Acts 20:35). Economic reciprocity and familial community were hallmarks of the earliest Christians of the New Testament period.

The material concern of Jesus traced through this *libellus* is consonant with a need-based understanding of economy, but opposes the exploitation of human beings through debt or the greed of commerce. Can it be that Jesus' economic concerns and values may help Christian cultures to redefine economic ends in an age of greed and global capitalism? Where indeed can the deeper wells of humane concern be found to irrigate a new order of economic justice? These will be among the great ethical questions for the twenty-first century.

4. Bellah, "Max Weber and World-Denying Love," 283.

5. Oakman, *The Political Aims of Jesus*, 84–94, 114–18; on this distinction, see Hauck, "Μαμωνᾶς."

Bibliography

Applebaum, Shimon. "Economic Life in Palestine." In *The Jewish People in the First Century: Historical Geography, Political History, Social, Cultural and Religious Life and Institutions*, edited by S. Safrai and M. Stern, 2:631–700. Compendia Rerum Iudaicarum Ad Novum Testamentum, section 1. Philadelphia: Fortress, 1976.

—. "Judaea as a Roman Province; Countryside as a Political and Economic Factor." In *Aufstieg und Niedergang der römischen Welt*, II.8:355–96. Berlin: de Gruyter, 1977.

Austin, M. M., and P. Vidal-Naquet. *Economic and Social History of Ancient Greece: An Introduction.* Berkeley: University of California Press, 1977.

Bagnall, Roger, and Peter Derow. *Greek Historical Documents: The Hellenistic Period.* Sources for Biblical Study 16. Chico, CA: Scholars, 1981.

Bailey, Kenneth E. *Poet and Peasant: A Literary Cultural Approach to the Parables in Luke.* Grand Rapids: Eerdmans, 1976.

—. *Through Peasant Eyes: More Lucan Parables, Their Culture and Style.* Grand Rapids: Eerdmans, 1980.

Bandstra, Andrew J. "The Original Form of the Lord's Prayer." *Calvin Theological Journal* 16 (1981) 15–37.

Barr, James. "Abba Isn't Daddy." *Journal of Theological Studies* 39 (1988) 28–47.

Barrera, Albino. *Biblical Economic Ethics: Sacred Scripture's Teachings on Economic Life.* Lanham, MD: Lexington, 2013.

—. *Market Complicity and Christian Ethics.* Cambridge: Cambridge University Press, 2011.

Barrois, A. "Debt, Debtor." In *Interpreter's Dictionary of the Bible*, edited by George Arthur Buttrick, 1:809–10. Nashville: Abingdon, 1962.

Bauer, Walter. *A Greek English Lexicon of the New Testament and Other Early Christian Literature.* Translated by William F. Arndt, F. Wilbur Gingrich and Frederick W. Danker. 2nd ed. Chicago: University of Chicago Press, 1979.

Bauer, Walter, and Frederick W. Danker. *A Greek English Lexicon of the New Testament and Other Early Christian Literature.* Based on Walter Bauer's Griechisch-deutsches Wörterbuch zu den Schriften des Neuen Testaments und der frühchristlichen Literatur, 6th ed., edited by Kurt Aland and Barbara Aland, with Viktor Reichmann and on previous English editions by William F. Arndt, F. Wilbur Gingrich, and Frederick W. Danker. 3rd ed. Chicago: University of Chicago Press, 2000.

Baumgardt, David. "Kaddish and the Lord's Prayer." *Jewish Bible Quarterly (Dor LeDor)* 19 (1991) 164–69.

Bellah, Robert N. "Max Weber and World-Denying Love: A Look at the Historical Sociology of Religion." *Journal of the American Academy of Religion* 67 (1999) 277–304.

Benoît, Pierre, Józef T. Milik, and Roland de Vaux. *Les Grottes de Murabbaʿat.* 2 vols. Discoveries in the Judean Desert 2. Oxford: Clarendon, 1961.

Betz, Hans Dieter. *The Sermon on the Mount.* Hermeneia. Minneapolis: Fortress, 1995.

Birnbaum, Philip, editor. *Daily Prayer Book.* New York: Hebrew Pub. Co., 1949.

Black, Matthew. *An Aramaic Approach to the Gospels and Acts.* 3rd ed. Reprinted, with an Introduction by Craig A. Evans. Peabody, MA: Hendrickson, 1998.

Blackman, Philip. *Mishnayoth.* 6 vols. London: Mishna Press, 1951–1955.

Blau, Ludwig. "Der Prosbol im Lichte der griechischen Papyri und der Rechtsgeschichte." In *Festschrift zum 50 jährige Bestehen der Franz-Josef-Landesrabbinerschule in Budapest*, edited by Ludwig Blau, 96–151. Budapest: Alexander Kohut Memorial Foundation, 1927.

Botha, F. J. "Recent Research on the Lord's Prayer." *Neotestamentica* 1 (1967) 42–50.

Brooke, George J. "The Lord's Prayer Interpreted through John and Paul." *Downside Review* 98 (1980) 298–311.

Brown, Francis, S. R. Driver, and Charles A. Briggs. *A Hebrew and English Lexicon of the Old Testament.* London: Oxford University Press, 1907.

Brown, John Pairman. "Prometheus, the Servant of Yahweh, Jesus: Legitimation and Repression in the Heritage of Persian Imperialism." In *The Bible and the Politics of Exegesis*, edited by David Jobling, et al., 109–25. Cleveland: Pilgrim, 1991.

Brown, Peter. *Through the Eye of a Needle: Wealth, the Fall of Rome, and the Making of Christianity in the West, 350–550 AD.* Princeton: Princeton University Press, 2012.

Brueggemann, Walter. "Trajectories in Old Testament Literature and the Sociology of Ancient Israel." *Journal of Biblical Literature* 98 (1979) 161–85.

Bruggen, Jacob van. "The Lord's Prayer and Textual Criticism." *Calvin Theological Journal* 17 (1981) 78–87.

Brunt, Peter. "Josephus on Social Conflicts in Roman Judaea." *Klio* 59 (1977) 149–53.

———. *Social Conflicts in the Roman Republic.* New York: Norton, 1971.

Bultmann, Rudolf. *The Theology of the New Testament.* Vol. 1. Translated by Kendrick Grobel. New York: Scribner, 1951.

Carney, Thomas F. *The Economies of Antiquity: Controls, Gifts and Trade.* Lawrence, KS: Coronado, 1973.

———. *The Shape of the Past: Models and Antiquity.* Lawrence, KS: Cornado, 1975.

Charlesworth, James H., editor. *The Old Testament Pseudepigrapha.* Vol. 1, *Apocalyptic Literature and Testaments.* Garden City, NY: Doubleday, 1983.

———. *The Old Testament Pseudepigrapha.* Vol. 2, *Expansions of the "Old Testament" and Legends, Wisdom and Philosophical Literature, Prayers, Psalms, and Odes, Fragments of Lost Judeo-Hellenistic Works.* Garden City, NY: Doubleday, 1985.

Chen, Tim. "American Household Credit Card Debt Statistics: 2014." Online: http://www.nerdwallet.com/blog/credit-card-data/average-credit-card-debt-household.

Childe, V. Gordon. *What Happened in History?* With a new Foreword by Professor Grahame Clark. Harmondsworth, UK: Penguin, 1964.

Chilton, Bruce. *The Temple of Jesus: His Sacrificial Program within a Cultural History of Sacrifice.* University Park: Pennsylvania State University Press, 1992.

Christian, David. *This Fleeting World: A Short History of Humanity.* Great Barrington, MA: Berkshire, 2008.

Cicero, Marcus Tullius. *De officiis.* Translated by Walter Miller. Loeb Classical Library. Cambridge: Harvard University Press, 1956.

Clark, Colin, and Maurine Haswell. *The Economics of Subsistence Agriculture.* 4th ed. New York: St. Martin's, 1970.

Collins, John J. "Early Jewish Apocalypticism." In *The Anchor Bible Dictionary*, edited by David Noel Freedman, 1:282–88. New York: Doubleday, 1992.

Coote, Robert B., and Mary P. Coote. *Power, Politics, and the Making of the Bible: An Introduction.* Minneapolis: Fortress, 1990.

Correns, Dietrich. *Schebiit. Vom Sabbatjahr: Text, Übersetzung und Erklärung.* Die Mischna: Text Übersetzung und ausführliche Erklärung. Berlin: Töpelmann, 1960.

Cox, Harvey. "The Market Is God: Living in the New Dispensation." *The Atlantic* March 1999, 18. Online: www.theatlantic.com/magazine/archive/1999/03/the-market-as-god/306397/?single_page=true.

Cross, Frank M. "Reconstruction of the Judean Restoration." *Journal of Biblical Literature* 94 (1975) 4–18.

Crossan, John Dominic. *The Birth of Christianity: Discovering What Happened in the Years Immediately after the Execution of Jesus.* San Francisco: HarperSanFrancisco, 1998.

———. *The Greatest Prayer: Rediscovering the Revolutionary Message of the Lord's Prayer.* San Francisco: HarperOne, 2011.

———. *The Historical Jesus: The Life of a Mediterranean Jewish Peasant.* San Francisco: HarperSanFrancisco, 1991.

Cyster, R. F. "The Lord's Prayer and the Exodus Tradition." *Theology* 64 (1961) 377–81.

Dalman, Gustaf. *The Words of Jesus.* Translated by D. M. Kay. Edinburgh: T. & T. Clark, 1902.

————. *Die Worte Jesu.* 2nd ed. Leipzig: Hinrichs, 1930.

Daly, Herman, and John B. Cobb, Jr. *For the Common Good: Redirecting the Economy toward Community, the Environment, and a Sustainable Future.* 2nd ed. Boston: Beacon, 1994.

Danby, Herbert. *The Mishnah: Translated from the Hebrew with Introduction and Brief Explanatory Notes.* Oxford: Oxford University Press, 1933.

Davies, W. D., and Dale C. Allison. "Excursus: The Lord's Prayer: Matthew 6.9–13 = Luke 11.2–4." In *Matthew,* 590–617. International Critical Commentary. Edinburgh: T. & T. Clark, 1988.

Deissmann, Adolf. *Bible Studies.* Translated by Alexander Grieve. 1909. Reprinted, Winona Lake, IN: Alpha, 1979.

————. *Light From the Ancient East: The New Testament Illustrated by Recently Discovered Texts from the Graeco-Roman World.* Rev. ed. Translated by L. R. M. Strachan. 1927. Reprinted, Eugene, OR: Wipf & Stock, 2004.

Derrett, J. Duncan M. "Law in the New Testament: The Parable of the Unjust Judge." *New Testament Studies* 18 (1971) 178–91.

de Ste. Croix, G. E. M. *The Class Struggle in the Ancient Greek World: From the Archaic Age to the Arab Conquests.* Ithaca, NY: Cornell University, 1981.

Dodd, C. H. *The Parables of the Kingdom.* Rev. ed. New York: Scribner, 1961.

Donahue, John. "Tax Collectors and Sinners: An Attempt at an Identification." *Catholic Biblical Quarterly* 33 (1971) 39–61.

Duling, Dennis C. *The New Testament: History, Literature, and Social Context.* 4th ed. Belmont, CA: Wadsworth/Thomson, 2003.

Duling, Dennis C., and Norman Perrin. *The New Testament: Proclamation and Parenesis, Myth and History.* 3rd ed. Fort Worth, TX: Harcourt Brace College, 1994.

Dyck, Bruno. *Management and the Gospel: Luke's Radical Message for the First and Twenty-First Centuries.* New York: Palgrave Macmillan, 2013.

Eissfeldt, Otto. *The Old Testament: An Introduction.* Translated by Peter R. Ackroyd. Harper & Row, 1965.

Elliott, John H. "Jesus the Israelite was Neither a 'Jew' nor a 'Christian': On Correcting Misleading Nomenclature." *Journal for the Study of the Historical Jesus* 5.2 (2007) 119–54.

————. *What Is Social-Scientific Criticism?* Guides to Biblical Scholarship. Minneapolis: Fortress, 1993.

Eusebius. *Ecclesiastical History.* Translated by Kirsopp Lake and J. E. L. Oulton. Loeb Classical Library. Cambridge: Harvard University Press, 1973–1975.

Fiensy, David A. *Christian Origins and the Ancient Economy.* Eugene, OR: Cascade Books, 2014.

Finley, Moses I. *The Ancient Economy.* Sather Classical Lectures 43. Berkeley: University of California Press, 1973.

Fitzmyer, Joseph A. *The Gospel according to Luke.* 2 vols. AB 28, 28A. Garden City, NY: Doubleday, 1981–1985.

Foerster, W. "Ἐπιούσιος." In *Theological Dictionary of the New Testament*, edited by Gerhard Kittel, 2:590–99. Translated by Geoffrey W. Bromiley. Grand Rapids: Eerdmans, 1964.

Francis, Pope. *Apostolic Exhortation Evangelii Gaudium, Of the Holy Father Francis to the Bishops, Clergy, Consecrated Persons and the Lay Faithful on the Proclamation of the Gospel in Today's World.* Rome: Libreria Editrice Vaticana, 2013.

Freedman, H., and Maurice Simon, eds. *Midrash Rabbah.* New York: Soncino, 1939.

Freyne, Seán. *Galilee from Alexander the Great to Hadrian 323 B.C.E. to 135 C.E.* Wilmington, DE: Michael Glazier, 1980.

Frizzell, Sam. "Americans Are Taking on Debt at Scary High Rates." *Time,* 19 Feb. 2014. Online: http://time.com/8740/federal-reserve-debt-bankrate-consumers-credit-card.

Furnish, Victor Paul. *Theology and Ethics in Paul.* Nashville: Abingdon, 1968.

Ginzberg, E. *Studies in the Economics of the Bible.* Philadelphia: Jewish Publication Society, 1932.

Glatzer, Nahum, editor. *The Passover Haggadah with English Translation Introduction and Commentary. Based on the Commentaries of E. D. Goldschmidt.* 3rd ed. New York: Schocken, 1979.

Goodman, Martin. "The First Jewish Revolt: Social Conflict and the Problem of Debt." *Journal of Jewish Studies* 33 (1982) 417–27.

———. *State and Society in Roman Galilee, A.D. 132–212.* Totowa, NJ: Rowman & Allanheld, 1983.

Goodspeed, Edgar J. *As I Remember.* New York: Harper, 1953.

Gouldner, Alvin. "The Norm of Reciprocity." In *Friends, Followers, and Factions: A Reader in Political Clientelism*, edited by Steffen W. Schmidt et al., 28–43. Berkeley: University of California, 1977.

Graeber, David. *Debt: The First 5,000 Years.* Brooklyn: Melville, 2011.

Grant, Frederick C. *The Economic Background of the Gospels.* 1926. Reprinted, New York: Russell & Russell, 1973.

Hamel, Gildas. *Poverty and Charity in Roman Palestine, First Three Centuries C.E.* Near Eastern Studies 23. Berkeley: University of California Press, 1990.

Hanson, K. C. "The Economy of Galilean Fishing and the Jesus Tradition." *Biblical Theology Bulletin* 27 (1997) 99–111.

———. "'How Honorable!' 'How Shameful!' A Cultural Analysis of Matthew's Makarisms and Reproaches." *Semeia* 68 (1994[96]) 81–111.

———. "Jesus and the Social Bandits." In *The Social Setting of Jesus and the Gospels,* edited by Wolfgang Stegemann, Bruce J. Malina, and Gerd Theissen, 283–300. Minneapolis: Fortress, 2002.

Hanson, K. C., and Douglas E. Oakman. *Palestine in the Time of Jesus: Social Structures and Social Conflicts.* 2nd ed. Minneapolis: Fortress, 2008.

Hauck, Friederich. "Μαμωνας." In *Theological Dictionary of the New Testament*, edited by Gerhard Kittel and translated by G. W. Bromiley, 4:388–90. Grand Rapids: Eerdmans, 1967.

———. "Οφειλω." In *Theological Dictionary of the New Testament*, edited by Gerhard Friedrich and translated by G. W. Bromiley, 5:559–66. Grand Rapids: Eerdmans, 1967.

Hemer, Colin J. "*Epiousios.*" *Journal for the Study of the New Testament* 22 (1984) 81–94.

Herzog, William R. II. *Jesus, Justice, and the Reign of God a Ministry of Liberation.* Louisville: Westminster John Knox, 2000.

Horsley, Richard A. "Jesus, Itinerant Cynic or Israelite Prophet?" In *Images of Jesus Today*, edited by James H. Charlesworth and W. P. Weaver, 68–97. Valley Forge, PA: Trinity, 1994.

Horsley, Richard A., and John S. Hanson. *Bandits, Prophets, and Messiahs: Popular Movements at the Time of Jesus.* San Francisco: Harper & Row, 1985.

Houlden, J. L. "The Lord's Prayer." In *The Anchor Bible Dictionary*, edited by David Noel Freedman, 4:356–62. New York: Doubleday, 1992.

Hunt, A., and C. Edgar. *Select Papyri.* Vol. 2: *Non-literary Papyri.* Loeb Classical Library. Cambridge: Harvard University Press, 1956.

Jacobson, Arland D. *The First Gospel: An Introduction to Q.* 1992. Reprinted, Eugene, OR: Wipf & Stock, 2005.

Jastrow, Marcus. *Dictionary of the Targumim, the Talmud Babli and Yerushalmi, and the Midrashic Literature.* 2 vols. 1903. Reprinted, New York: Pardes, 1950.

Jenkins, Philip. "The Next Christianity." *The Atlantic* 10 (2002). Online: http://www.theatlantic.com/past/docs/issues/2002/10/jenkins.htm.

Jeremias, Joachim. "Ηλ(ε)ιας." In *Theological Dictionary of the New Testament*, edited by Gerhard Kittel, 2:928–41. Grand Rapids: Eerdmans, 1964.

———. *Jerusalem in the Time of Jesus.* Translated by F. H. Cave and C. H. Cave. Philadelphia: Fortress, 1969.

———. *The Lord's Prayer.* Translated by John Reumann. Philadelphia: Fortress, 1980.

———. "The Lord's Prayer in Modern Research." *Expository Times* 71 (1960) 141–46.

———. *New Testament Theology.* Vol. 1: *The Proclamation of Jesus.* Translated by John Bowden. New York: Scribner, 1971.

———. *The Parables of Jesus.* Translated by S. H. Hooke. 2nd ed. New York: Scribner, 1972.

———. *The Prayers of Jesus.* Studies in Biblical Theology 2/6. Naperville, IL: Allenson, 1967.

Jones, A. H. M. "Taxation in Antiquity." In *The Roman Economy; Studies in Ancient Economic and Administrative History*, edited by P. A. Brunt, 151–85. Oxford: Blackwell, 1974.

Josephus. *Josephus in Nine Volumes.* Translated by H. St. J. Thackeray, Louis H. Feldman et al. Loeb Classical Library. Cambridge: Harvard University Press, 1976.

Kelly, J. N. D. *Early Christian Creeds.* London: Longman, 1972.

Kiley, Mark. "The Lord's Prayer and Other Prayer Texts from the Greco-Roman Era: A Bibliography." In *The Lord's Prayer and Other Prayer Texts from the Greco-Roman Era,* edited by James H. Charlesworth et al., 101–257. Valley Forge, PA: Trinity, 1994.

Kippenberg, Hans von. *Religion und Klassenbildung im Antiken Judäa.* Studien zur Umwelt des Neuen Testaments 14. Göttingen: Vandenhoeck & Ruprecht, 1978.

Klausner, Joseph. *Jesus of Nazareth: His Life, Times, and Teaching.* Translated by Herbert Danby. New York: Macmillan, 1925.

Kloppenborg (Verbin), John S. *Excavating Q: The History and Setting of the Sayings Gospel.* Minneapolis: Fortress, 2000.

———. *The Formation of Q: Trajectories in Ancient Wisdom Collection: With a New Preface.* Studies in Antiquity and Christianity. Harrisburg, PA: Trinity, 1999.

———. "Literary Convention, Self-Evidence and the Social History of the Q People." *Semeia* 55 (1992) 77–102.

———. *Q Parallels: Synopsis, Critical Notes, and Concordance.* Foundations and Facets. Sonoma, CA: Polebridge, 1988.

———. "The Sayings Gospel Q: Recent Opinion on the People Behind the Document." *Currents in Research: Biblical Studies* 1 (1993) 9–34.

Koffmahn, Elisabeth. *Die Doppelurkunden aus der Wüste Juda: Recht und Praxis der jüdischen Papyri des 1. und 2. Jahrhunderts n. Chr. samt Übertragung der Texte und deutscher Übersetzung.* Studies on the Texts of the Desert of Judah 5. Leiden: Brill, 1968.

Krentz, Edgar. "Epideiktik and Hymnody: The New Testament and Its World." *Biblical Research* 40 (1995) 50–97.

Lachs, Samuel Tobias. "The Lord's Prayer." In *A Rabbinic Commentary on the New Testament,* 117–24. Hoboken, NJ: Ktav, 1987.

Lenski, Gerhard E. *Power and Privilege: A Theory of Social Stratification.* New York: McGraw-Hill, 1966.

Lewis, Naphtali. *Life in Egypt under Roman Rule.* Oxford: Clarendon, 1983.

Lewis, Naphtali, and Meyer Reinhold, editors. *Roman Civilization: Selected Readings.* Vol. 2, *The Empire.* New York: Columbia University Press, 1955.

Liddell, H., R. Scott, and H. Jones. *A Greek English Lexicon with A Supplement.* Oxford: Clarendon, 1968.

Lightfoot, John. *A Commentary on the New Testament from the Talmud and Hebraica.* 4 vols. 1859. Reprinted, Grand Rapids: Baker, 1979.

MacMullen, Ramsay. *Roman Social Relations: 50 B.C. to A.D. 284.* New Haven: Yale University Press, 1974.

Malina, Bruce J. "Interpretation: Reading, Abduction, Metaphor." In *The Bible and the Politics of Exegesis: Essays in Honor of Norman K. Gottwald on His*

Sixty-Fifth Birthday, edited by David Jobling, Peggy L. Day and Gerald T. Sheppard, 253–66. Cleveland: Pilgrim, 1991.

———. *The New Testament World: Insights from Cultural Anthropology*. 3rd ed. Louisville: Westminster John Knox, 2001.

———. "'Religion' in the World of Paul." *Biblical Theology Bulletin* 16 (1986) 92–101.

———. *The Social World of Jesus and the Gospels*. London: Routledge, 1996.

Manson, T. W. *The Sayings of Jesus*. London: SCM, 1949.

Martínez, Florentino García. *The Dead Sea Scrolls Translated: The Qumran Texts in English*. Translated by Wilfred G. E. Watson. 2nd ed. Leiden: Brill, 1996.

McCane, Byron R. "'Let the Dead Bury Their Own Dead': Secondary Burial and Matt 8:21–22." *Harvard Theological Review* 83 (1990) 31–43.

Meier, John P. *A Marginal Jew: Rethinking the Historical Jesus*. Vol. 2: *Mentor, Message, and Miracles*. Anchor Bible Reference Library. New York: Doubleday, 1994.

Metzger, Bruce M. *A Textual Commentary on the Greek New Testament: A Companion Volume to the United Bible Societies' Greek New Testament*. 3rd ed. London: United Bible Societies, 1975.

Miller, Stuart S. *Studies in the History and Traditions of Sepphoris*. Studies in Judaism in Late Antiquity 37. Leiden: Brill, 1984.

Moor, Johannes C. de. "The Reconstruction of the Aramaic Original of the Lord's Prayer." In *The Structural Analysis of Biblical and Canaanite Poetry*, edited by W. van der Meer and J. C. de Moor, 397–422. JSOTSup 74. Sheffield: JSOT Press, 1988.

Moulton, James H., and Wilbert F. Howard. *A Grammar of the New Testament Greek*. Vol. 2, *Accidence and Word Formation, with an Appendix on Semitisms in the New Testament*. Edinburgh: T. & T. Clark, 1920.

Moulton, James H., and George Milligan. *The Vocabulary of the Greek Testament*. 1930. Reprinted, Grand Rapids: Eerdmans, 1985.

Neusner, Jacob. *From Politics to Piety: The Emergence of Pharisaic Judaism*. 1973. Reprinted, Eugene, OR: Wipf & Stock, 2003.

Neyrey, Jerome H. "My Lord and My God": The Divinity of Jesus in John's Gospel." In *Society of Biblical Literature Seminar Papers*, ed. Kent Harold Richards, vol. 25, 152–71. Atlanta: Scholars Press, 1986.

———. *Render to God: New Testament Understandings of the Divine*. Minneapolis: Fortress, 2004.

———, ed. *The Social World of Luke-Acts: Models for Interpretation*. Peabody, MA: Hendrickson, 1991.

Nicholas, Barry. *An Introduction to Roman Law*. Clarendon Law Series. Oxford: Clarendon, 1962.

Oakman, Douglas E. "The Ancient Economy." In *The Social Sciences and New Testament Interpretation*, edited by Richard L. Rohrbaugh, 126–43. Peabody, MA: Hendrickson, 1996. Reprinted in Oakman, *Jesus and the Peasants*, 53–69.

————. "The Archaeology of First-Century Galilee and the Social Interpretation of the Historical Jesus." In *Society of Biblical Literature 1994 Seminar Papers*, edited by Eugene H. Lovering, Jr., 220–51. Atlanta: Scholars, 1994. Reprinted in Oakman, *Jesus and the Peasants*, 245–79.

————. "BTB Readers Guide: The Ancient Economy in the Bible." *Biblical Theology Bulletin* 21 (1991) 34–39.

————. "Economics of Palestine." In *Dictionary of New Testament Background*, edited by Craig A. Evans and Stanley E. Porter, 303–8. InterVarsity, 2000.

————. "Galilee." In *The Eerdmans Dictionary of the Bible*, edited by David Noel Freedman, 478–80. Grand Rapids: Eerdmans, 2000.

————. "Jesus and Agrarian Palestine: The Factor of Debt." In *Society of Biblical Literature 1985 Seminar Papers*, edited by Kent Harold Richards, 57–73. Atlanta: Scholars, 1985. Reprinted in Oakman, *Jesus and the Peasants*, 11–32. Revised version is chapter 1 in this volume.

————. *Jesus and the Economic Questions of His Day*. Studies in the Bible and Early Christianity 8. Lewiston, NY: Mellen, 1986.

————. *Jesus and the Peasants*. Matrix: The Bible in Ancient Mediterranean Context 4. Eugene, OR: Cascade Books, 2008.

————. "The Lord's Prayer in Social Perspective." In *Authenticating the Words of Jesus*, edited by Bruce Chilton and Craig A. Evans, 137–86. NTTS 28.1. Leiden: Brill, 1999. Reprinted in Oakman, *Jesus and the Peasants*, 199–242. Revised version is chapter 2 in this volume.

————. "Models and Archaeology in the Social Interpretation of Jesus." In *Social-Scientific Models for Interpreting the Bible: Essays by the Context Group in Honor of Bruce J. Malina*, edited by John J. Pilch, 102–31. Biblical Interpretation Series 53. Leiden: Brill, 2001. Reprinted in Oakman, *Jesus and the Peasants*, 245–79.

————. *The Political Aims of Jesus: Peasant Politics in Herodian Galilee*. Minneapolis: Fortress, 2012.

————. "The Radical Jesus: You Cannot Serve God and Mammon." *BTB* 34 (2004) 122–29.

————. "Rulers' Houses, Thieves, and Usurpers: The Beelzebul Pericope." *Forum* 4.3 (1988) 109–23. Reprinted in Oakman, *Jesus and the Peasants*, 118–31.

————. "Was Jesus a Peasant? Implications for Reading the Samaritan Story (Luke 10:30–35)." *Biblical Theology Bulletin* 22 (1992) 117–25. Reprinted in Oakman, *Jesus and the Peasants*, 164–80.

Oxfam. *Working for the Few: Political Capture and Economic Inequality*. Oxford: Oxfam GB, 2014. Online: http://www.oxfam.org/sites/www.oxfam.org/files/bp-working-for-few-political-capture-economic-inequality-200114-en.pdf.

Perrin, Norman. *Rediscovering the Teaching of Jesus*. New York: Harper & Row, 1976.

Piketty, Thomas. *Capital in the Twenty-first Century*. Translated by Arthur Goldhammer. Cambridge, MA: Belnap, 2013.

Pilch, John J. *The Cultural Dictionary of the Bible.* Collegeville, MN: Liturgical, 1999.

Polanyi, Karl. *The Great Transformation: The Political and Economic Origins of Our Time.* Boston: Beacon, 1957.

———. *The Livelihood of Man.* Edited by Harry W. Pearson. Studies in Social Discontinuity. New York: Academic, 1977.

Preisigke, Friedrich. *Fachwörter des öffentlichen Verwaltungsdienstes Ägyptens in den griechischen Papyrusurkunden der ptolemäisch-römischen Zeit.* Göttingen: Vandenhoeck & Ruprecht, 1915.

Priene Inscription, Greek text and translation by Frank Finn. Online: http://www.artsci.wustl.edu/~fkflinn/Priene%20Inscription.html

Pritchard, James B. *Ancient Near Eastern Texts Relating to the Old Testament.* 3rd ed. Princeton: Princeton University Press, 1969.

Randerson, James. "World's Richest 1% Own 40% of All Wealth, UN Report Discovers." *The Guardian* 6 December 2006. Online: www.guardian.co.uk/money/2006/dec/06/business.internationalnews.

Redfield, Robert. "The Social Organization of Tradition." In *The Little Community and Peasant Society and Culture*, 40–59. Chicago: Phoenix Books, 1960.

Riesner, Rainer. "Bethany beyond the Jordan." In *The Anchor Bible Dictionary* edited by David Noel Freedman, 1:703–5. New York: Doubleday, 1992.

Robbins, Vernon K. *Exploring the Texture of Texts: A Guide to Socio-Rhetorical Interpretation.* Valley Forge, PA: Trinity, 1996.

Robertson, R. G. "Ezekiel the Tragedian." In *The Old Testament Pseudepigrapha*, edited by James H. Charlesworth, Vol. 2: *Expansions of the "Old Testament" and Legends, Wisdom and Philosophical Literature, Prayers, Psalms and Odes, Fragments of Lost Judeo-Hellenistic Works.* Garden City, NY: Doubleday, 1985.

Robinson, James M., Paul Hoffmann, and John S. Kloppenborg. *The Critical Edition of Q.* Hermeneia Supplements. Minneapolis: Fortress, 2000.

Rostovtzeff, Michael. *The Social and Economic History of the Hellenistic World.* 3 vols. Oxford: Clarendon, 1941.

———. *The Social and Economic History of the Roman Empire.* 2 vols. Oxford: Clarendon, 1957.

Sandel, Michael J. "What Isn't for Sale." *The Atlantic* April 2012. Online: www.theatlantic.com/magazine/archive/2012/04/what-isnt-for-sale/308902.

———. *What Money Can't Buy: The Moral Limits of Markets.* New York: Farrar, Straus & Giroux, 2012.

Sanders, E. P. *The Historical Figure of Jesus.* London: Penguin, 1993.

Schottroff, Luise, and Wolfgang Stegemann. *Jesus and the Hope of the Poor.* Translated by Michael J. O'Connell. Maryknoll, NY: Orbis, 1986.

Schrenk, Gottlob. "Βουλομαι." In *Theological Dictionary of the New Testament*, edited by Gerhard Kittel, 1:629–37. Translated by Geoffrey W. Bromiley. Grand Rapids: Eerdmans, 1964.

————. "Θέλημα." In *Theological Dictionary of the New Testament*, edited by Gerhard Kittel, 3:52–62. Translated by Geoffrey W. Bromiley. Grand Rapids: Eerdmans, 1965.

Scott, James C. *Weapons of the Weak: Everyday Forms of Peasant Resistance.* New Haven: Yale University Press, 1985.

Scott, S. P. *The Civil Law, Including the Twelve Tables, the Institutes of Gaius, the Rules of Ulpian, the Opinions of Paulus, the Enactments of Justinian, and the Constitutions of Leo.* Translated from the original Latin, edited, and compared with all accessible systems of jurisprudence ancient and modern. Cincinnati: Central Trust, 1932.

Seesemann, H. "Πεῖρα." In *Theological Dictionary of the New Testament*, edited by Gerhard Friedrich, 6:23–36. Translated by Geoffrey W. Bromiley. Grand Rapids: Eerdmans, 1968.

Sherwin-White, A. N. *Roman Society and Roman Law in the New Testament.* The Sarum Lectures 1960–1961. Grand Rapids: Baker, 1963.

Smith, B. T. D. "Lord's Prayer." In *Interpreter's Dictionary of the Bible*, edited by George Arthur Buttrick, 3:155. Nashville: Abingdon, 1962.

————. *The Parables of the Synoptic Gospels: A Critical Study.* Cambridge: Cambridge University Press, 1937.

Smith, Dan. *The Penguin State of the World Atlas.* 8th ed. New York: Penguin, 2008.

Stählin, Gustav. "Χήρα." In *Theological Dictionary of the New Testament*, edited by Gerhard Kittel and Gerhard Friedrich, 9:440–65. Grand Rapids: Eerdmans, 1974.

Stegemann, Ekkehard S., and Wolfgang Stegemann. *The Jesus Movement: A Social History of Its First Century.* Translated by O. C. Dean Jr. Minneapolis: Fortress, 1999.

Stegemann, Wolfgang. *The Gospel and the Poor.* Translated by Dietlinde Elliott. Philadelphia: Fortress, 1984.

Stendahl, Krister. "Matthew." In *Peake's Commentary on the Bible*, edited by Matthew Black and H. H. Rowley. London: Nelson, 1962.

Strack, Hermann L., and Paul Billerbeck. *Kommentar zum Neuen Testament aus Talmud und Midrasch.* 6 vols. 9th ed. Munich: Beck, 1986.

Tacitus, Cornelius. *The Histories; The Annals.* Translated by C. H. Moore and J. Jackson. 4 vols. Loeb Classical Library. Cambridge: Harvard University Press, 1925–1937.

Taussig, Hal. "The Lord's Prayer." *Forum* 4.4 (1988) 25–41.

Theissen, Gerd. *The Gospels in Context: Social and Political History in the Synoptic Tradition.* Translated by Linda M. Maloney. Minneapolis: Fortress, 1991.

————. *Sociology of Early Palestinian Christianity.* Translated by John Bowden. Philadelphia: Fortress, 1978.

Thucydides. *The History of the Peloponnesian War.* Translated by Richard Crawley. Revised by R. Feetham. In *Herodotus, Thucydides.* Edited by Robert

Maynard Hutchins, 6:349–593. The Great Books of the Western World. Chicago: Encyclopaedia Britannica, 1952.

Tillich, Paul. *The Protestant Era*. Translated by James Luther Adams. Chicago: Phoenix, 1957.

———. *The Socialist Decision*. Translated by Franklin Sherman. 1977. Reprinted, Eugene, OR: Wipf & Stock, 2012.

Torvend, Samuel. *Luther and the Hungry Poor: Gathered Fragments*. Minneapolis: Fortress, 2008.

Turner, Nicholas. *A Grammar of New Testament Greek*. Edinburgh: T. & T. Clark, 1963.

Udoh, Fabian Eugene. "Tribute and Taxes in Early Roman Palestine (63 BCE–70 CE): The Evidence from Josephus." Ph.D. dissertation, Duke University, 1996.

———. *To Caesar What Is Caesar's: Tribute, Taxes and Imperial Administration in Early Roman Palestine (63 B.C.E.–70 C.E.)*. Brown Judaic Studies 343. Providence, RI: Brown Judaic Studies, 2005.

Viviano, Benedict T. "The Gospel according to Matthew." In *The New Jerome Biblical Commentary*, edited by Raymond E. Brown, Joseph A. Fitzmyer and Roland E. Murphy, 630–74. Englewood Cliffs, NJ: Prentice Hall, 1990.

Weber, Max. *Economy and Society*. 2 vols. Edited by Guenther Roth and Claus Wittich. Translated by Ephraim Fischoff. Berkeley: University of California Press, 1978.

———. *The Sociology of Religion*. Introduction by Talcott Parsons. Translated by Ephraim Fischoff. Boston: Beacon, 1963.

Westcott, B. F., and F. J. A. Hort. *Introduction to the New Testament in the Original Greek, With Notes on Selected Readings*. New York: Harper, 1882.

Wolf, Eric R. "The Hacienda System and Agricultural Classes in San Jose, Puerto Rico." In *Social Inequality: Selected Readings*, edited by André Béteille, 172–90. Penguin Modern Sociology Readings. Baltimore: Penguin, 1969.

———. *Peasants*. Foundations of Modern Anthropology Series. Englewood Cliffs, NJ: Prentice Hall, 1966.

Wright, Addison G. "The Widow's Mites: Praise or Lament?" *Catholic Biblical Quarterly* 44 (1982) 256–65.

Young, Brad. *The Jewish Background to the Lord's Prayer*. Austin, TX: Center for Judaic–Christian Studies, 1984.

Zahavy, Tzvee. *Studies in Jewish Prayer*. Studies in Judaism. Lanham, NY: University Press of America, 1990.

Index of Ancient Documents